'THEORY INTO PRACTICE'

The Complete Practical Theory Of Outdoor Education And Personal Development

Peter Barnes

Thanks to;

Sue Towson for drawing the cover and giving her support and encouragement,
Brian Green and Douglas Weir for their help with the finance,
Malcolm Warwick for his patience and help with the printing,
Chris Loynes for his comments and suggesting the title
and everyone else who has helped with comments and suggestions.

(all other cover art work by the author)

Published by the - **Faculty of Education,**
University of Strathclyde,
Jordanhill Campus,
Glasgow. G133 1PP

Financed by the - **Scottish School of Sport Studies,**
Faculty of Education,
University of Strathclyde.

Printed by - **Reeds Limited,**
Penrith.

First published 1997.

(Chapter 3. 'All about leadership' is based on a chapter prepared by the author and Phil Woodyer for Marshall, D. 'Cave Leader's Handbook' - in preparation)

ISBN 1 900 743 302

CONTENTS;

(Except for chapter 1 there is no significance in the order of the chapters)

FIGURES;

INTRODUCTION;

At one time it was enough to take groups into the great outdoors and leave the impact of the environment, the experience of outdoor activities and the companionship of fellow group members to teach their own lessons. We know now that there is much more to outdoor education than that - and more to the point the paying public also know more and are asking for more. It is no longer enough to say 'Wow!' we now have to add on 'How?' and perhaps more importantly 'Why?'. This book is another aid, just as a map, a rope or a canoe is an aid, in helping to answer those questions.

The aim of this book is to present the popular theories used in outdoor education in a simple, concise and usable format. This is done in the hope that outdoor staff, facilitators, tutors, instructors, call them what you will, will use it as a resource to turn to rather than trawling through a mass of papers, articles, books and hearsay as they do at present. This book is not in any way an 'academic' or 'intellectual' text. Whilst it does deal with a number of heavy weight theories I have endeavoured to reduce the content of these down to the point where they become **practical theories**, if there is such a thing! It may be that you already know much, if not most, of what is written in these pages in which case those sections will serve as good *aides mémoire* but I sincerely hope that everyone will find something here that is new to them.

There are few original concepts in this book, there is very little new in education either in the classroom or in the outdoors, and I certainly make no great claims here. The true work has already been done by the thinkers and theorists who originally put the theories together and I freely acknowledge my debt to them.

Note that throughout this book I have randomly used the terms his and hers, he and she rather than try to corrupt the English language for the sake of being politically correct. I have referred to those people who work in the outdoors by a number of terms but most commonly 'instructors' an expression which I know will not find favour with everybody but it does seem the most suitable of generic terms. I have generally referred to those people on outdoor courses as 'students' or 'group members'.

I hope you find this book both useful and enjoyable.

Peter Barnes.

1. THE ART OF COMMUNICATION

Communication is central to any development experience although it is rarely addressed as a subject in its own right. This chapter looks at how people communicate and gives some simple pointers for effective communication.

HOW PEOPLE COMMUNICATE - The levels of communication.

The first thing to remember with communication is that people hold conversations at different levels of intimacy or depth, these are shown in figure i. Any instructor, or facilitator, needs to be aware of these levels because they hold the key not only to effective reviewing but also the effectiveness of much of the outdoor experience itself.

Figure i

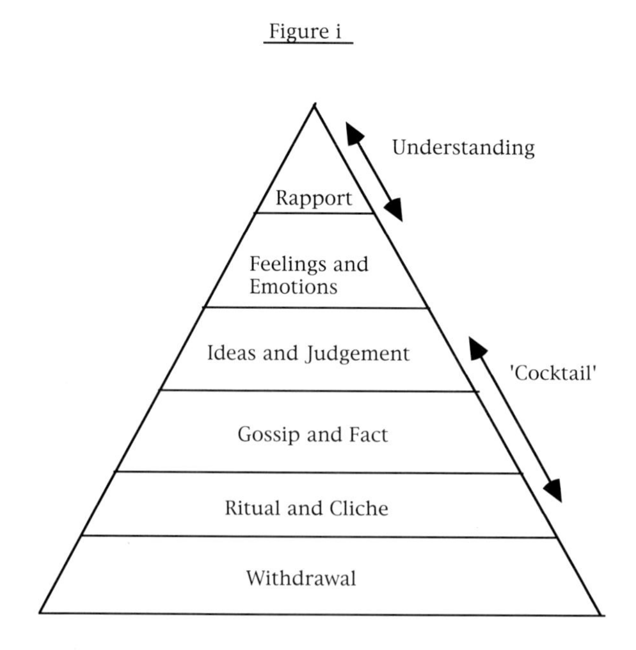

The levels of communication

The levels marked as 'cocktail' are essentially the components of so called polite conversation. The most famous cliché must be the expression 'how are you?' where no answer is really expected or indeed welcomed beyond a simple 'fine thanks, and you?'. Ritual is best expressed in the British tradition of discussing the weather with all and sundry. Moving up the scale, 'gossip and fact' although implying a more involved conversation still do not involve the speakers on a personal level.

The same is true of 'ideas and judgements' where although opinions may be expressed the feelings behind them are not. It is not until the 'feelings and emotion' level that true communication becomes apparent with 'rapport', which is essentially non-verbal, being the ultimate in communication where true understanding is reached. The level of rapport communication is rarely reached and almost inevitably will involve couples of long term standing. Married couples and established climbing partners are the obvious examples of this.

One of the most important factors of outdoor education is that it enables, or forces, students to leap several levels of communication and engage in feelings and emotions at a much earlier stage than would normally be expected.

The danger is that what may appear to be feelings and emotion can often be merely disguised ritual, for example a student when asked how she felt during an abseil may reply 'scared' without giving any thought to it because that is the expected response. A good reviewer will be able to see through this and move the conversation/ discussion to higher levels.

It is important to remember, however, that when engaging in 'feelings and emotions' level dialogue people are laying themselves open in a very personal manner. This may not always be necessary and should not be forced just because of a belief that outdoor courses involve high emotions. A team development course, for example, may not need to do more than dip into this level with the majority of the conversation being carried out at the top end of the ideas and judgement level.

The features of effective communication (B.T. 1997) are;

- It is a genuine **two-way** experience
- Both sides are **heard** and **understood** with both sides being **open**
- The atmosphere is **comfortable** enabling **important** things to be said
- The conversation/communication **makes a difference**

EFFECTIVE COMMUNICATION - How to ensure it works

A lot of conversation fails to achieve its objective and results in misunderstanding. The following five pointers are essential for establishing effective communication;

- Always think clearly before you start talking - **Engage brain before opening mouth!** Know what you are going to say and the objective of the conversation.

- Consider the timing of the conversation and the climate in which it is to take place. For example bringing up a person's failings when they are in floods of tears may well not be appropriate!

- How you say something can be as important as what you say. Consider the overtones of the conversation. Ask yourself how the recipient feels, try to put yourself in their shoes.

- Be aware of body language and your physical position, sitting behind a desk is an immediate barrier to communication for example. Likewise delivering an awkward message can be softened by sitting next to someone rather than standing in front of them with your hands on your hips. Body language such as folded arms (defensive) all makes a difference to communication.

- Communication is about listening as much as talking!

TWO-WAY COMMUNICATION - The key to success.

All good communication is a two way process and requires good listening skills as well as good talking skills. A good example of this is to watch a doctor interviewing a patient, note how she will hold her head slightly to one side to show that she is listening and encourage the patient with nods of the head and verbal prompts.

A good exercise to demonstrate the importance of two-way communication is to ask a group member to describe a complicated shape to his group. This should be done with no physical help, tell him to put his hands behind his back, and no questioning from the group. Next get him to describe another shape but this time the group can ask questions, this will, usually, be much more effective. This exercise also demonstrates how much we tend to use our hands in normal conversation.

2. LEARNING FROM THE OUTDOOR EXPERIENCE

There are a wide and enormously complex number of theories regarding how people learn, this book, however, deals specifically with how and why people learn on outdoor courses. It first looks at why the outdoors is seen as so effective for learning purposes. Following this the chapter looks at how people learn and then at self-perception.

THE OUTDOOR LEARNING EXPERIENCE - Why people learn.

Many students on outdoor courses will ask what is it about the outdoors that makes it so effective for learning and, even if they don't ask, a short introduction to learning in the outdoors should usually be part of any start of course briefing.

> The reason why the outdoors is used as a learning medium for personal and team development is because, as well as being fun, it is so powerful.

In straightforward terms the outdoor environment is powerful for a number of reasons, these are;

- **The outdoors is an alien experience.** For most people outdoor activities will be new and different to their everyday experiences. Some activities, such as caving, may be extremely so. This disorientation means that students are very receptive to learning as they have few references to past experience to help them.

- **The outdoors is an equaliser.** This manifests itself in a number of ways from a young offender realising that he has as much to offer as other members of his group to a manager realising that her secretary has hidden strengths which she herself does not possess.

- **The outdoors is fun.** This is an element often missed by people but it is a simple fact that people learn quickly if they are enjoying themselves.

- **Real consequences can be used as learning points.** It is very hard in hypothetical classroom situations to get people to accept the true consequence of their actions whereas in the outdoor environment every action has a good or bad consequence some of which can be unpleasant or uncomfortable - although on a course they should never be truly dangerous (although they may seem so).

- **Fears and challenges can be approached in a supportive environment.** Although a student might be very conscious of losing face in a work environment in the outdoors where most of his fellow group members are experiencing the same fears and concerns it is easier to be open about them. This is amplified by the natural bonding and mutual support that working together in the outdoors engenders

- **Everyday concerns are left behind.** Learning can be a difficult experience when everyday concerns such as work and financial issues are constantly at the back of a person's mind. By transferring the learning to the outdoor environment and thus detaching it from the 'real world' these concerns can be left behind.

- **Emotions are heightened.** In everyday life people tend to keep a tight rein on their emotions which usually acts as a strong barrier to any form of personal development. Outdoor activities bring emotions, both good and bad, to the surface enabling them to be experienced, shared and built on.

- **Communication is enhanced.** There is very little as effective as powerful shared experiences when trying to open up meaningful conversation. The powerful emotions and levelling of group members engendered by the outdoor experience means that conversation is often carried out at the 'feelings and emotions' level rather than the more normal 'cocktail' levels.

- **The very nature of the outdoors and outdoor activities means that powerful and highly memorable moments are experienced.** These moments, which are discussed next in this chapter, mean that not only will an experience be remembered for a long time but perception and with it, learning, is increased to an elevated level.

- **The outdoors is practical.**

  "What I hear - I forget,
  What I see - I remember,
  What I do - I learn." *Chinese proverb*

THE POWER OF THE OUTDOORS - Flow, magic moments and peak experience.

When people speak of the power of the outdoors they tend to be speaking of specific moments which were highly significant and memorable. These momentary experiences can be explained by the concepts of 'flow', 'magic moments' and 'peak experiences'. Although these three types of experience are often spoken of as though they are the same thing this is not strictly true although they are so closely linked that it often doesn't matter too much. In essence they can be thought of as;

- **Flow**; is a state which exists in a person when performing in an activity at a level which perfectly matches the physical and mental ability of the performer and where the 'performer' is totally identified with that activity to the exclusion of outside stimulation.

- **Magic moments**; tend to have more spiritual and emotional connotations than flow. They are often exemplified by feelings of 'quietness' and 'being at one' with nature or a deity or sharing with other people. Some people speak of magic moments as 'transcendence'

- **Peak experiences**; are strongly allied to flow in that performance is an important part of the experience; however emotion, which is largely detached from flow, plays a stronger role. To some extent peak experiences can be thought of as a combination of many of the aspects of flow and magic moments and therefore producing a more all-round feeling.

Of the three states flow is the most highly researched, notably by Csikszentmihayli (1990) who included rock climbers in his study of skilled performers which led to the initial concept of flow state. The features of flow include undivided task attention, a limited stimulus field, perceptions of personal control over the activity and clear goals.

Flow is not confined to highly skilled operators, it is a progressive state which reflects the right level of skill being matched to the right amount of challenge being experienced. A1 for example in figure ii, although at a low level of challenge has an appropriate level of skill and is thus in a state of flow, A4 although at a much higher challenge level has a higher level of skill to meet it and is thus also in a state of flow. A2 however, has a high level of skill which is not being met and is therefore in a state of boredom whilst A3 has the opposite problem being in a state of anxiety due to not having the required level of skills to meet the level of challenge. An important feature of flow that it is not stable, as skill level increases the individual will need to seek a higher level of challenge in order to return to a state of flow.

Figure ii

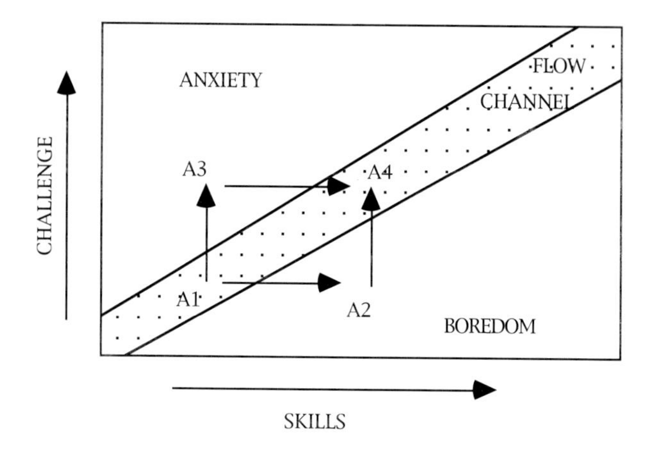

The Concept Of Flow

The main work on magic moments was done by Maslow (1959) who saw them as essentially spiritual in nature. Many outdoor instructors comment on 'magic moments' when they are at one with their group in relation to the activity and/or the environment. Such moments can be as simple and obvious as reaching the summit of a hill together or more intangible such as sharing stories after a meal. These moments tend to involve empathy with nature or sharing with close companions rather than the adrenaline rush of performance as in flow. Some instructors when involved with groups even go so far as to say that their work is sometimes a succession of magic moments and peak experiences with long periods of routine in between. Furthermore instructors often report that these moments are the aspect of the work that gives it meaning.

The importance of these powerful momentary experiences is that people will not only remember them for a long time but they can also be moments when all the lessons and experiences of an outdoor course 'come together' and make sense. An instructor cannot force these moments onto students but by providing the right activities at the right level (see chapter on risk) and at the right time she can provide the right circumstances for them to happen in.

HOW TO HELP PEOPLE LEARN - Using the senses.

People learn in a number of ways but which ever way is used all learning will make use of the six sense channels;

- Sight
- Hearing
- Smell
- Touch
- Taste
- Muscle-memory

The first key to really effective learning is to use as many of the sense channels as possible. Although sight is the most commonly used, and useful, of the sense channels, in skills training touch and muscle-memory also play a vital part. A second key to learning is that the learning process should be interesting, involving and motivate the students to want to learn.

To take an example from an outdoor course look at a caving session. The students are totally involved, it is impossible to stand back and watch when travelling through a cave! Hopefully the instructor will be making the trip as enjoyable and interesting as possible thereby encouraging the students motivation. All the sense channels, with the exception of taste, are involved at some stage. On the face of it caving should be a great learning experience. However there is one catch -

> 'Knowledge dispels fear,
> but when someone is too scared they forget all their knowledge'

No-one will learn anything if they are totally terrified. All instructors are familiar with the sensation of 'being gripped' basically this occurs when there is too much sensation and the body, and brain, freezes. Unlike being 'very scared' being 'gripped' is rarely, if ever, a useful learning experience and can be highly counter-productive.

Learning is most effective when **an action or material is presented in manageable parts.** This is the familiar breaking down of a technique into its parts that all instructors learn when training. There should be a period of consolidation, either mental or physical, between each part. Likewise the parts should follow a logical sequence and be placed within the context of the whole activity. An example of this would be that teaching someone how to belay but not telling them what belaying is for is unlikely to inspire their learning.

Following on from this there needs to be **a reason for learning**. Telling the group that they need to learn to belay because they will responsible for each other's safety is an obvious incentive for them to learn. The instructor should always, however, be aware of why people are on a course in the first place as this may have a direct link to their desire and willingness to learn. As mentioned in the section above, the fact that the outdoor experience holds real consequences for actions is one of the reasons why it is such a powerful learning tool.

It is not always a natural process to **associate facts and ideas**. This explains the student who simply cannot accept that a climbing rope is strong enough to hold him even though he has been told all the relevant figures. Using analogy, metaphor or simple examples are all effective ways of overcoming this, for example, rather than say 'this rope will hold so many kilograms' say 'this rope would easily lift this entire group' or 'because of the way this rope is made it is much stronger than this old style heavy rope'. The association of ideas makes the facts easier to accept.

If students are well **motivated and interested** in the course then obviously the learning process is much easier. In any instance, however, the following techniques will always make learning more interesting;

- **Questions and answers**; are far more effective and interesting than one way 'lecturing'.

- **Discussion**; is often needed because few subjects will be cut and dried with no issues to be resolve. Discussion also helps students to not only learn from the instructor but also from each other.

- **Exercises**; are a good way of maintaining interest. Physical practice of each part of a new skill is far more effective than waiting in silence and then practising the whole skill. Repetition of an exercise also overcomes the inherent short term normal memory by making use of the much more effective muscle-memory.

- **Variety**; because variety is the spice of life! However learning one new skill immediately after learning another one can be counter-productive as the earlier skill will be forgotten. There needs to be alternation between old and new skills.

THE STAGES OF LEARNING - The use of learning cycles.

The most common learning model used in outdoor education is that of learning cycles. The popularity of these is two-fold, firstly they are simple, elegant yet effective and, secondly, they show clearly the progression of learning which typifies outdoor courses. There are many forms of learning cycles but essentially, in recent terms, they all evolve from the circular learning pattern of Kolb (1971) shown in figure iii. The true originator of the experiential learning cycle is, however, John Dewey (1938) who is widely regarded as the 'father' of experiential education.

Figure iii

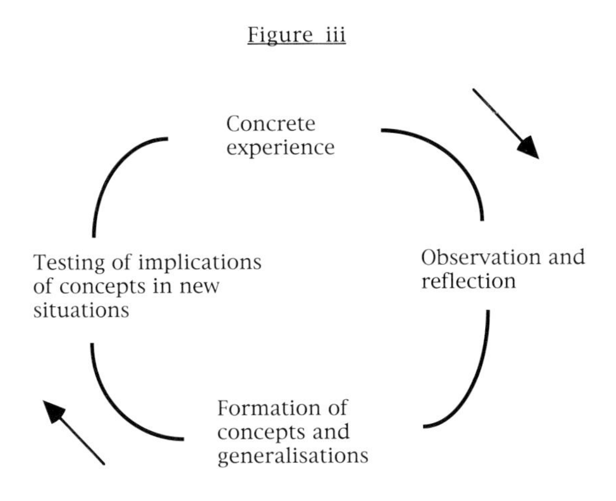

Kolb's Circular Learning Pattern

The four stages in Kolb's cycle can be simply described as -

Something happens - What happened? - What did it mean? - What now?

For sheer simplicity, elegance and effectiveness there is little that can beat this model. Not only is this model seen as the basis for experiential learning it can also be used as the structure for reviewing activities and tasks (see chapter on reviewing). It is also very effective when used for briefing students at the start of an exercise or activity. Kolb's circular pattern has formed the basis for many other circular patterns, for example Outward Bound staff have traditionally used a circle of **Plan, Do, Review** to describe the learning process on their courses. This simple and effective model is often expanded into a spiral to give the model shown in figure iv.

Figure iv

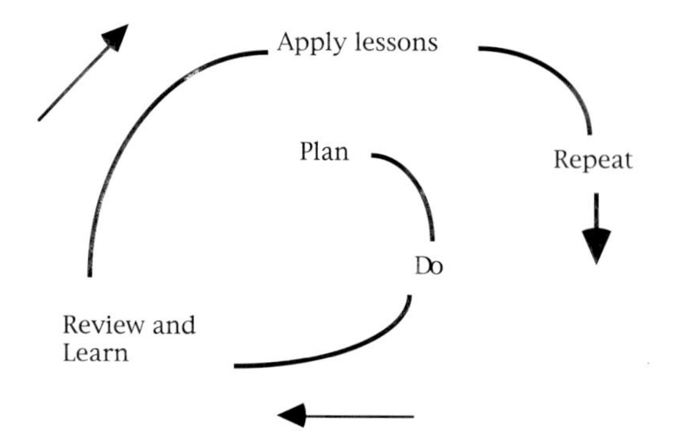

An example of a learning spiral model

Figure v

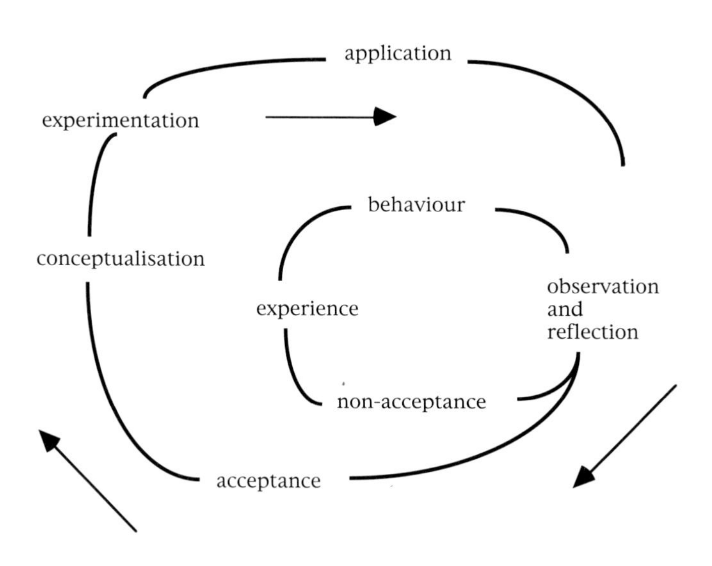

Developmental Spiral Model

The spiral model is now rapidly replacing the traditional circular learning model which could be taken to imply that skills are not transferable to situations outside of the circle. A much more elaborate spiral, based on Tuson's (1994) model, is shown in figure v. This model shows that behaviour is followed by a period of reflection at which point a decision is made. If the behaviour is accepted than a traditional learning cycle of 'what happened' and through to 'what next' and implementing those lessons is followed. If the behaviour is rejected then the inner circle continues until an increase in experience allows that behaviour to become acceptable and the larger spiral to be entered.

HOW PEOPLE PERCEIVE THEMSELVES - Johari's window.

One of the prime objectives of an outdoor course is to get people to see themselves for what they really are. It is only when this self-honesty is achieved that truly effective personal development can take place. One very powerful model to help with demonstrating this self-perception is Johari's window. The word Johari is a derivative of the names of Joseph Luft and Harry Ingham who developed the model as a technique for reducing inter-personal conflict in the sixties (Luft, 1961). In its purest form the model is shown, in figure vi, as a four windowed box.

Figure vi

	You are aware of others	You are not aware of others
You are aware of yourself	**OPEN SELF**	**HIDDEN SELF**
You are not aware of yourself	**BLIND SELF**	**UNDISCOVERED SELF**

Johari's Window

The key element of the window is that it relates to self and how that individual, 'you' in this example, perceives others perception of himself. The common technique of using the window to show the perceptions of others is not strictly correct but is a development of the original idea and is dealt with later. In the standard model the four elements are;

- **Open self**; in which you are aware of how you affect others and you are also aware of others impact on you. In addition others are aware of your knowledge. In this scenario this is nothing hidden and, therefore, little risk of interpersonal conflict.

- **Hidden self**; where you are aware of the your feelings and intentions, however you are not aware of the others reaction to you. In this scenario you do not reveal your true feelings in order to avoid conflict. This may lead to mistrust on the part of others.

- **Blind self**; in this situation you are aware of others but you are unaware of how you may be affecting them. It may be that you are unintentionally irritating them. If you are open to feedback this situation can be resolved otherwise it may lead to conflict.

- **Undiscovered self**; here you are not only unaware of how you affect others but you are also unaware of the others motives and intentions. This is a volatile situation with plenty of scope for interpersonal misunderstanding and conflict.

It can be seen that one of the difficulties with the Johari's window model is that it requires a degree of convoluted thought in order to really get to grips with its true implications. Probably because of this it has been generally adapted to the model shown in figure vii. This model is not talking about a person's own perception of self and others but rather how things may be viewed from both the perspective of self and of others.

The features of this model are rather simpler to grasp, for example, an individual may be unaware of an irritating habit, or 'blind spot', which is obvious to others and needs to be pointed out to him. The Johari's window, in both its forms, makes the elegant learning point that -

We don't always know everything about ourselves - and we don't usually know how others see us.

Figure vii

	Others know	Others do not know
You know	**ARENA** (things you know and others know)	**FACADE** (things you know and others don't know)
You do not know	**BLIND SPOT** (things others know and you don't know)	**UNKNOWN** (things you don't know and other's don't know)

The developed model of Johari's window

Everyday life can be said to exist in the 'arena' and 'facade' areas with most people being private about their innermost thoughts and feelings in much the same way as the everyday conversation is carried on at the 'cocktail' level.

The aim of an outdoor course is to move a student's self-perception through the 'blind spot' and ultimately into the 'unknown' area.

It is by doing this that the self-development element of an outdoor course starts to work. Many things have to come together for people to move into the 'unknown' area but the most important of them is for a person to be honest with him or herself.

"Only within yourself exists that other reality for which you long.
I can give you nothing that has not already its being within yourself.....
All I can give you is the opportunity, the impulse, the key .....
to make your own world visible"
Herman Hesse (1927) Steppenwolf

KNOWING OUR OWN SKILLS - Kolb and Johari combined.

The Kolb learning cycle and Johari's window can be combined to give the model in figure viii. In simple terms this model makes the point that we have to know that we can't do something, 'conscious incompetence', before we can learn the skills needed to do it well.

Figure viii

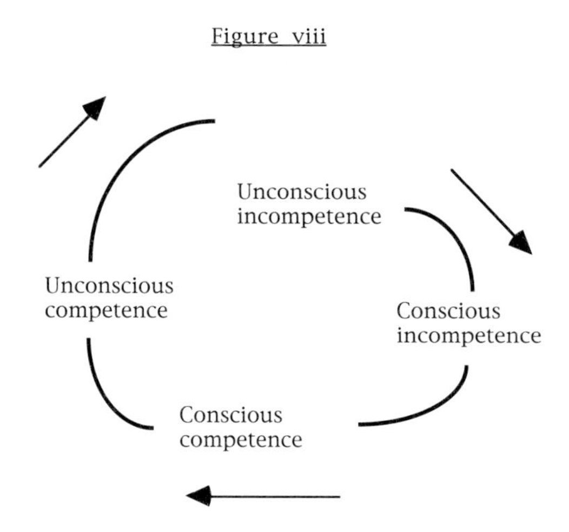

The Kolb learning cycle and Johari's window combined model

This cycle can be related to the gathering of experience and confidence on an outdoor course. To give an example, someone may attend a course having no idea about rock climbing (unconscious incompetence) they will try it, find it difficult and the instructor will have to show them what they are doing wrong (conscious incompetence). By learning these lessons and with practice they will develop the skills of a rock climber (conscious competence) and with further experience those skills will become instinctive (conscious competence).

Not only can this model be applied to hard skills such as rock climbing the same lessons can be applied to learning about personal habits, traits and abilities and the self-perception needed to do that. It emphasises the point that learning can often be a difficult experience because the first stage has to be admitting that either something is unknown or that something needs changing.

3. ALL ABOUT LEADERSHIP

This chapter looks at leadership not only from the point of view of the instructor but also at how the leadership responsibility is transferred to group members. It examines where power comes from and how much power to use as well as the practical issues of what a leader should know and the responsibilities of a leader. It concludes by looking at 'Action Centred Leadership' probably the most popular leadership model in use at the moment.

Leadership of any sort is a difficult subject and outdoor leadership is particularly so. In few sports or activities are so many demands made on the leader, he or she has a wide number of roles to play. These roles can include safeguarding a group without killing the joy of exploration and discovery, educating without becoming a bore and reassuring without being condescending. There is a lot more to being a leader than just having a knowledge of the outdoors and personal expertise as a climber, canoeist or caver. One aspect that is touched on in this chapter is the need for an outdoor leader to exercise **judgement**, this is usually taken as the ability to make decisions based on experience, knowledge, qualification, personal skill and 'gut instinct'. Judgement is at the heart of all outdoor leadership decisions and is often only acquired through making mistakes and learning from them. More than anything else it is this aspect of leadership that requires experience and maturity.

WHERE POWER COMES FROM - The bases of power

Before leadership can be fully understood it is well to appreciate where the power to be a leader comes from. There are four sources of power which are generally known as the **bases of power**. These power bases are; **resource, expert, position** and **charisma power.**

- **Resource Power.** The essence of resource power is that the leader has it within his or her power to give, or withhold, some form of reward. In an industrial or business context this power base can be the ability to provide, and increase or decrease, wages, promotion and ultimately employment itself. The resources controlled by the outdoor leader can be as tangible as the type of activity provided or more subtle rewards such as praise or approval.

- **Expert Power.** This is usually the most acceptable form of power because people are able to rationalise why the 'expert' is in charge. For expert power to work the group must acknowledge and respect that a person has the necessary expertise. This is the reason why bluffing to cover up for a lack of knowledge almost inevitably ends up with loss of control over a group.

- **Position Power.** There are two sources of position power, sometimes known as 'legitimate power', these are nominated and democratic. Nominated power implies some form of authority conferred in the leader. This will usually be the group leader with the power conferred in them by virtue of the job. Democratic power is where a group of people have elected a leader for various possible reasons. It is important to note that position power can be hard to maintain, in many cases it relies on being able to call on one or more of the other forms of power base, such as expert power. It is absolutely vital that people who have position power invested in them never give way to the "because I said so and I'm in charge" type of leadership or they will soon find themselves out of power!

- **Charisma Power.** This is perhaps the most sought after, and the most abused, form of power. The reason for this is that charisma power is seen as a validation of the person rather than the position. The source of charismatic power is in the personality of the person wielding it. This personality need not be loud, a calm manner can often be a vital asset allowing this type of leader to act as an effective co-ordinator. People who lack true charisma power, but aspire to it, are prone to dominate, rather than lead, the group through loudness or physical presence. At its best this type of domination is disruptive and at its worst can be highly counterproductive.

It can be seen that an outdoor leader should have 'expert' power as an absolute minimum. A leader should never underestimate how nervous, apprehensive or even out and out scared inexperienced students can be, it is their trust and confidence in the leader that allows novices to overcome these fears. This trust and confidence can be built up in a number of ways, it can also just as easily be destroyed in a number of ways. A group will automatically assume, quite rightly, that the leader is more experienced and more capable than themselves. This assumption will be reinforced by a leader establishing good practice right from the start of an activity or course.

The group will be looking to see that a leader;

- Knows the environment/area he or she is working in;
- Knows the equipment;
- Knows the activity;
- Knows his or her capabilities;
- Knows how to relate to the group;
- And; **is enthusiastic.**

In addition to 'expert' power an outdoor leader would normally have 'position' power simply because they are 'the leader', they may well, however, need to call on 'charisma' power if there are 'characters' in the group who need either winning over or reassuring. Finally 'resource' power is the ultimate trump card where if things are not working out the leader always has the power to abandon or change the trip or activity.

HOW MUCH POWER TO USE - The continuum of leadership.

To a large extent how much power to use is the key, and the secret, of good leadership. It can be summed up by figure ix which is based on the work of Tannerbum and Schimdt (1968)

This figure makes it quite clear that at the left of the continuum the leader enjoys total, autocratic, leadership. This is usually a very safe style of leadership but can be stifling for the group. At the other extreme the leader has abdicated leadership and the group is allowed to make its own mistakes. There is a time and a place for this style of leadership as much as for autocratic leadership, however it can quickly lead to unsafe situations. It may seem as if the ideal is a position somewhere between these two extremes but the truth is that the amount of leadership a good leader displays can be swinging back and forwards on an almost constant basis. A quick litany describing the leadership continuum is that, going from left to right of the model, the leader - **tells, sells, tests, consults, joins, delegates** and finally **abdicates**.

The prime rule to remember when handing over leadership is, however;

Authority can be delegated but responsibility never can.

Figure ix

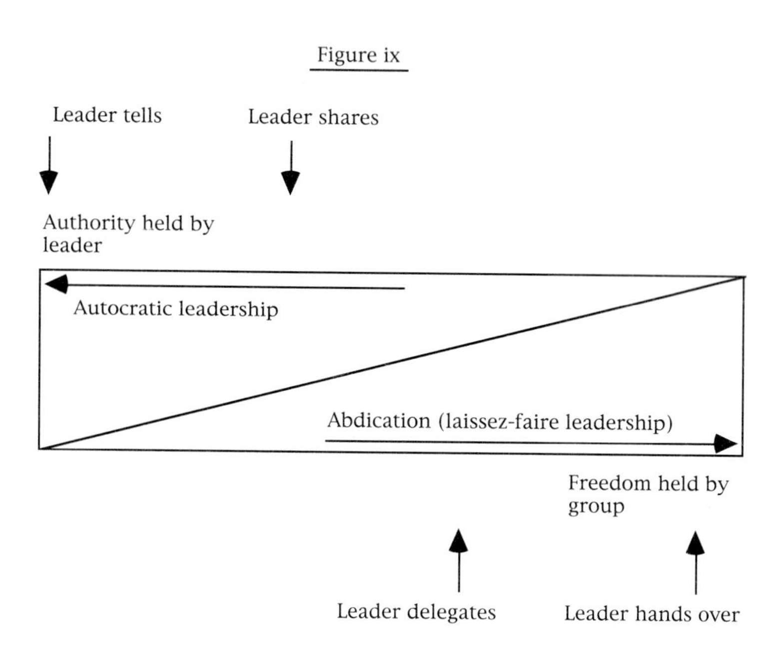

The Leadership Continuum

The aim of any leader should be to hand over as much authority as is sensible and appropriate but always be in a position to grab it back as soon as it is necessary.

The continuum of leadership can also be reflected in the style of leadership adopted. These styles, based on a theme developed by Phil Woodyer, can be summed up as shown in figure x.

Figure x

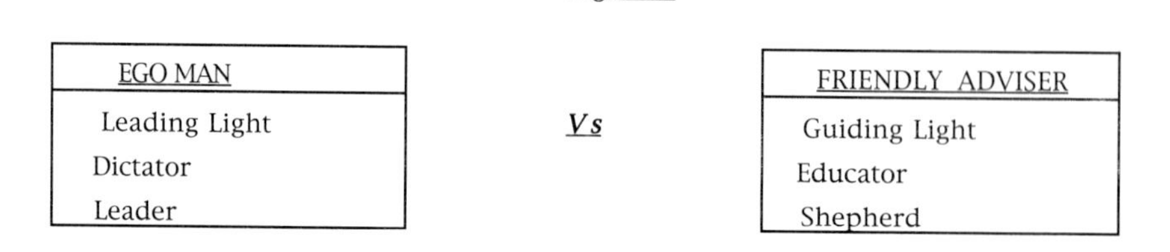

Styles of leadership

These roles may often seem contradictory but should rather be viewed as complimentary and switched between as appropriate. It is worth asking where you fit into these roles when working as an outdoor leader or instructor.

Are you an 'Ego Man' dragging all and sundry along with you to do what you want to do, to impress your party with your vast feats of daring, your immunity to pain and cold water and your vast knowledge? Or are you the 'Friendly Adviser', leading by suggestion, guiding your party to self-discovery and self-awareness? 'Ego Man' may impress many of his party but will not interest many of them in the activity in question unless his ego is tempered with a certain amount of sympathy for the needs and fears of the party. 'Friendly Advisor' may well switch his party on to what they are doing and the environment around them, but he may also switch them off permanently if at certain times he does not assert his authority when danger threatens.

Do you lead the party from the front, always in one line in single file behind you or do you encourage them to go off and discover for themselves, keeping a wary eye on all. Again it depends on the environment, the activity and the group. Often the best place for the leader to be with a group is at the head pointing out all dangers and features and arriving first at any area which may be hazardous. However, there are many occasions when a group should be allowed to go on their own or take it in turns to lead. The key to allowing this is firstly you should know the location well enough to be sure that there are no hazards that the group may encounter and, secondly, to brief them on what they may encounter and give them strict limits on the length of their exploration. They should not be allowed to become too spread out and no one should be allowed to shoot off ahead. Ideally this handing over of leadership should only occur where you can instantly resume control if necessary.

No doubt you would argue that you do not entirely fit into either side of the table and this is as it should be. A persons style of leadership grows from their personality and there are elements of all of these extremes in all of us. Good leadership comes from knowing when to use them, with which individuals and groups and in which situations. Being a leader is not always easy.

"The ultimate measure of a man is not where he stands in moments of comfort and convenience, but where he stands during challenge and controversy"
Martin Luther King

WHAT A LEADER SHOULD KNOW - The rules of leadership.

There are some simple 'rules' of leadership which are always worth bearing in mind for anyone leading groups. The same rules can also be applied to students when placed in leadership positions. The rules are;

- **A leader needs to be fair and must never be seen to be biased.**

  This should go without saying but it can be difficult if some of the group are pleasant and easy to get on with and others are difficult. A leader should be careful how he distribute tasks and responsibilities. or even how much time he spends talking to certain people.

  The instructor must ensure that when a student has been nominated as leader that he or she does not show bias towards friends in the group. This can be very difficult for a student, the danger is that some members of the group may become excluded.

- **Leadership is not about ego.**

  It cannot be denied that leadership, especially outdoor leadership, acts as a major ego boost. This is particularly the case with younger leaders. A sensible leader will not deny this fact but be aware of it and question the way they act.

  The instructor will need to know when students are unable, or too immature, to handle the responsibility of leadership. It is up to him to keep on top of the situation.

- **Good leadership is often the ability to delegate effectively.**

- **...... however, ultimate responsibility can never be delegated.**

  These are perhaps the most important points that the leader, must remember. It may be that she is working on building up levels of leadership and/or teamwork amongst the group and in order to do this has handed over the running of the group to the group members. **Authority can be delegated but responsibility never can.** In order to delegate authority it is important that a leader has established herself as the responsible leader of the group before handing over the running of the group.

Often a student leader jumps in with the 'follow me, this is how we will do it' technique. One of the hard rules of leadership is that others may have better ideas which need to be both listened to and encouraged. A good leader is exemplified by the ability to encourage and use other peoples skills and ideas. The blame, however, cannot be passed down if those skills and ideas fail to work.

- **A leaders behaviour towards members of the opposite sex must not be capable of being misconstrued.**

This should, hopefully, go without saying but it is very easy to fall into certain traps. For example, if teaching skills a leader must be careful not to always use a group member of the opposite sex to demonstrate on. A leader's behaviour must be beyond reproach, often even the most innocent of actions can be misconstrued and at best undermine their leadership or at worst get them into very real trouble.

If an instructor is on top of a group this situation should not occur with students. It doesn't matter if the group are school children or senior managers. If the behaviour of certain members of the group is causing offence or distress to others it is up to the instructor to put a stop to it although obviously the technique used to do this will vary with the situation.

- **Criteria and standards set by the leader must be made clear from the start.**

A leader can't make up the rules as they go along. The standards must be set at the start of a course and stuck to. This is particularly important when it comes to safety matters and the delegation of leadership.

Nominated student leaders should be encouraged to make themselves clear from the outset by giving a good briefing to the group and acting in a consistent manner.

- **Leaders must not be critical of others without very good reason and rarely, if ever, in public.**

If a leader is harsh towards a member of your group in public the other group members will usually quickly 'gang up' in support of them. If there is a need to criticise somebody they should be taken to one side.

A leader should also be very aware of the danger of discussing or criticising students without their knowledge to fellow group members. This can easily be taken as 'backstabbing'.

The art of giving feedback is one that needs to be learnt and should usually take place in a controlled environment. It is perhaps wise not to allow students to be too critical of each other, at least not in the early stages of a course.

- **The leader sets an example.**

It can be hard but in front of a group the leader must live by their own rules. Students are very quick to notice if they are in the river getting soaked and the leader is on the bank telling them that it won't hurt, likewise the leader can't always delegate the washing up!

This rule is less important for students as group members will not be looking to each other to set an example in quite the same way as they look to the instructor. In leadership terms the rule about fair delegation above is more important for the group. Having said that; the essence of outdoor courses is often in the 'shared experience' and it can be hard to get a nominated leader to stand back from an activity.

- **And finally - A leader learns the names of the group!**

Not only does this make for a more pleasant time but in a moment of crisis it may make all the difference between being understood or being ignored.

A group will never develop in either leadership or team spirit if they do not know each others names. There are a whole variety of games which can be used to foster this .

WHEN IT COMES TO THE CRUNCH - the leader's responsibilities.

This section is aimed specifically at the outdoor leader or instructor. A leader not only takes responsibility for the group but through that action also, automatically, assumes responsibility for many other things. These responsibilities are shown in figure xi.

Figure xi

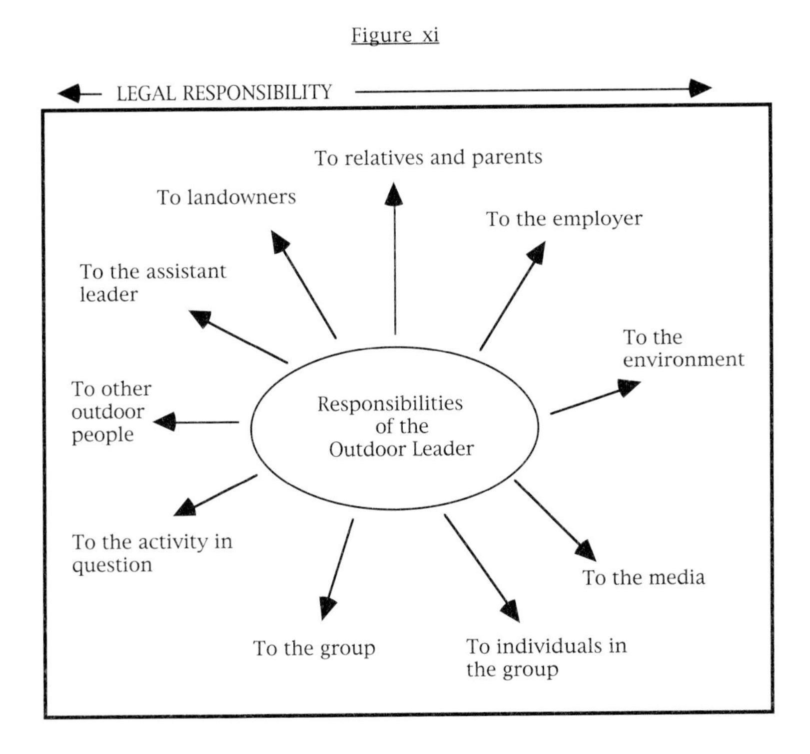

The Responsibilities Of An Outdoor Leader

Many of these responsibilities are self evident and few instructors will need reminding of them. Because of their importance however, and at the acknowledged risk of patronising outdoor staff, they are presented here in some detail.

- **Relatives/parents.**

    The close relatives of the group a leader will be working with are very interested in their qualities as a leader because they are handing their relative's lives into his or her care.

- **Other outdoor people.**

  Whilst out with a group it is almost inevitable that instructors will come into contact with other people using the outdoors. They will obviously have their own opinions of organised parties and may regard groups as a nuisance. It is always best to be polite and considerate; however, remember that groups, usually, have as much right to be there as they have.

- **The media.**

  Sadly it is unlikely that many outdoor people will come across the media in a beneficial way, unfortunately if they do come into contact with them it will often be because there has been an accident of some sort. A leader should always attempt to be polite to reporters but **never** give the names of group members involved in any incident. If the accident doesn't actually involve the leader or his group it is wise to resist being roped in as an 'instant expert', a firm 'I wouldn't like to comment' is usually the best approach.

- **The environment.**

  Not only should the leader maintain environmental discipline but they should also attempt to educate the group members. The pressure on nearly all of the outdoor environment in Great Britain is now tremendous and any parties which use it must be taught to respect its fragility.

- **The employer.**

  Whilst leading a group a leader is not only an advertisement for herself but also for her employer. Likewise complaining about an employer to a group is unprofessional and unacceptable.

- **The group.**

  To a large extent a leader's main responsibility is to the group in their care. This may sound so obvious that it hardly needs saying but in many ways it is the easiest of responsibilities to neglect. The first consideration should always be; is the activity in question a suitable activity for the group, and if it is, is the venue also suitable. An easy trap to fall into is to take a group to an area that the leader is keen on rather than an area that is suitable for them.

- **Landowners.**

  Ultimately many areas in this country can only be used with the goodwill of the landowner. Often all a landowner may see of a group is a badly parked minibus, litter and gates left open. Consideration should always be a leader's watchword, farmers have a living to make as much as they do.

- **The sport or activity.**

  Many outdoor activities, unfortunately and unfairly, have a reputation as dangerous and somewhat bizarre pastimes. One of the only contacts that most people will have with the outdoors is as a member of an organised party. In other words the only outdoor person that many people will ever meet is the instructor. Hopefully some of the group members will carry on with the activity in question but often the trip will be a one off experience and it is important, therefore, to present the sport in its best light.

- **Individuals in the group.**

  This can be the hardest of all the responsibilities, a group is made up of individuals - a fact which is sometimes easy to overlook! The group as a whole may be working well together and having a great time but if one person is stumbling along at the back, cold, wet and terrified then the leader is failing. There is no right or wrong solution to a situation like this occasionally however, it needs to be recognised that some outdoor activities just aren't suitable for everybody and plans adjusted accordingly.

- **The assistant leader.**

  It may sound strange that the instructor is responsible for the assistant leader if they have one. However they are not only responsible for his or her safety but also responsible for their actions.

Overall Legal Responsibilities;

Outdoor leaders are faced with an ever increasing amount of legal responsibilities and legislation. This should not in any way put anyone off being a leader, most instructors will find that they can fulfil their responsibilities with a little common sense and without too much difficulty. The notable legal points to be aware of include;

- **In Loco Parentis.**

In Loco Parentis means quite simply 'in place of the parent', it implies that any person who has charge of young people, usually taken as under sixteen, has the same duty of care for them as a responsible parent would have. This is a serious and major responsibility for any leader as it means that they have total care, and must accept total responsibility, for any young people they may work with.

- **Duty of Care.**

Whether there is a legal contract or not any leader can be said to have a duty of care for the members of his group. This need not be an organised group in the commercial sense, if a leader sets him or her self up as an expert in the eyes of the group they assume the responsibility that goes with it.

- **Activity Centres (Young Persons' Safety) Act 1995.**

This act which is operated through the 'Adventure Activities Licensing Regulations 1996' and by the 'Adventure Activities Licensing Authority' (AALA) means that by October 1997 all providers of specified outdoor activities must have been inspected and licensed. In essence if a leader takes people **under the age of eighteen** on most outdoor activities in return for payment then the chances are that these regulations will apply to them, or, more likely, their employer. To operate without a license is a criminal offence.

There is a voluntary licensing scheme run in parallel with the mandatory scheme for those who wish to be licensed but are not covered by the licensing regulations.

- **Minibus Driving.**

Whilst not strictly part of a leaders job most instructors will have to drive a minibus and should be aware of the minibus regulations. These can be complex but in general state that anyone, the driver is responsible, driving a vehicle of more than eight seats which has not been registered for educational or charitable purposes needs the appropriate license or permit.

- **Equipment.**

New European directives on outdoor equipment mean that it will be an offence to use any piece of safety equipment, such as helmets, for commercial purposes which do not carry EU approval. This can be recognised by the 'EC' mark. These regulations also put a time restriction on how long equipment can be used for. Normal UIAA standards will, however, also still apply.

TO BE AN EFFECTIVE LEADER - Action centred leadership

One of the most popular leadership models used by outdoor leaders is that developed by John Adair (1988) which shows that effective leadership needs to take into account three things; group needs, task needs and individual needs. This is usually shown by the three circles model shown in figure xii.

In essence this model shows that there are three aspects to leadership which must interact, the point at which the circles cross, before that leadership can be said to be truly effective. These aspects are **achieving the task, developing the individual** and **building the team.**

Figure xii

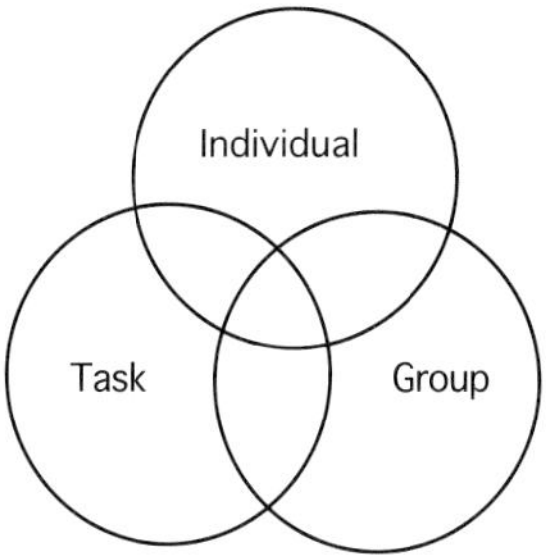

Individual

Task

Group

The classic three circle model of Action Centred Leadership

The reason for these three areas can be seen as the chained need, or aim, to achieve a **task** through the use of a **team** of people who are all **individuals**. This aim is achieved through using the key actions shown in figure xiii. In addition to its leadership function, action centred leadership is a useful indicator of good team work.

Figure xiii

Key Actions	**Task**	**Team**	**Individual**
Define objectives	• Identify tasks and constraints	• Involve team • Share commitment	• Clarify objectives • Gain acceptance
Plan	• Establish priorities • Check resources • Decide • Set Standards	• Consult • Encourage Ideas and actions • Develop suggestions • structure	• Assess skills • Set targets • Delegate
Brief	• Brief the team • Check understanding	• Answer questions • Obtain feedback	• Listen • Enthuse
Support and monitor	• Report progress • Maintain standards • Discipline	• Co-ordinate • Reconcile conflict	• Advise • Assist/reassure • Recognise Effort • Counsel
Evaluate	• Summarise progress • Review objectives • Replan if needed	• Recognise success • Learn from failure	• Assess performance • Appraise • Guide, train and develop

The key features of Action Centred Leadership

4. RISK

Risk is a central part of the outdoor process for two completely different reasons. Firstly it forms an ever present backdrop to almost all outdoor activities, it introduces the question of safety and the minimising of risk to acceptable levels. Secondly it is the element of risk that not only gives many outdoor activities their excitement but also their potential for use in self-development. This chapter looks at risk from both of these viewpoints. It explains how risk is defined and quantified and then looks at how risk is individual and different for different people.

Whilst this book does not set out to be a comprehensive work on safety in the outdoors, there are many good books on the subject, risk and safety cannot be separated. There are a large number of factors which contribute to safe practice, notably;

- attitude of mind/ethos
- procedures; formal and informal
- equipment
- responsibility
- legislation
- leadership

Of these perhaps the most important is attitude of mind coupled with good leadership. All the other factors are, to some extent, features of the physical practice of an outdoor centre, the attitude of the instructors, however, is not only less tangible but also less influenced by external factors. Whilst bad procedures, bad equipment, bad equipment and so on can all be overcome by good, conscientious staff the opposite is not true. The best system using the best equipment will still be unsafe if the person in charge doesn't care about safety.

WHAT IS RISK - A definition.

Before risk can be defined it must be understood that there are two fundamentally different types of risk associated with outdoor activities. These are **Perceived Risk** and **Actual Risk**.

Perceived risk is how the risk involved in an activity is **felt** by the person doing the activity whilst actual risk is the risk that is present in **reality**.

Bearing this distinction in mind, risk is best defined (Wharton, 1996) as being the;

LIKELIHOOD OF HARM OCCURRING x SEVERITY OF THAT HARM

To take an example of this, using an arbitrary a scale of ten, rock climbing in a normal outdoor centre setting can be seen to be low risk -

RISK FROM ROCK CLIMBING = 1 x 9 =9

This is because whilst the severity of the harm that might occur is high (9) a person might die, the actual likelihood of that harm occurring is very low (1). Ghyll scrambling, or gorge walking, on the other hand is a much higher risk -

RISK FROM GHYLL SCRAMBLING = 4 x 6 =24

This occurs because, even though the likely harm that might happen to a student is somewhat lower (4) the likelihood of that harm occurring is much higher (6) giving a higher total risk. In other words the activity which seems safer is actually the more dangerous one. This is not at all unusual in the outdoor world, think of the so called low level activities often used with younger children such as assault courses or mountain biking. Whilst they might seem safe they are in reality more risky than kayaking, caving or rock climbing where much more direct control is exercised by the instructor.

It is important to emphasise that so far we have only mentioned **physical harm**, the importance of **psychological harm**, or trauma, is just as real when considering outdoor activities and can even, in some cases, have longer lasting effects. Most aspects of physical harm can also be applied to psychological harm.

Another common usage use of the word risk is in the difference between **Objective Risk** and **Subjective Risk**. In simple terms the difference between the two is that the first one is talking about risks which are outside of the control of a group leader whilst the second can, usually, be controlled. An example of objective risk would be avalanches which, although dangerous areas can be avoided, cannot be controlled.

THE RISK IN SMALL THINGS - The accident equation.

Another way of looking at levels of risk is to use the accident equation developed by Simon Priest (1990)

Figure xiv

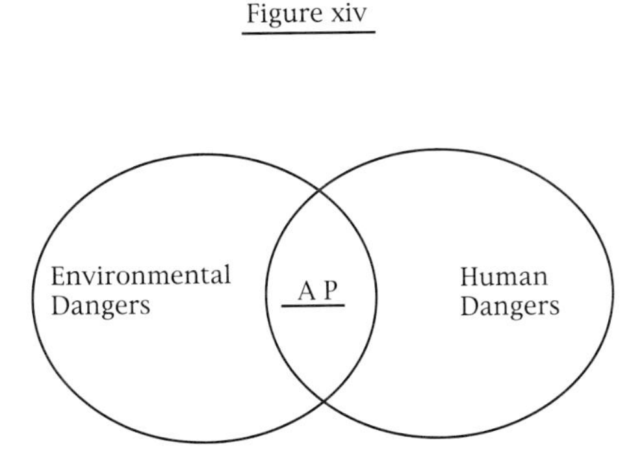

The Accident Equation

This makes the assumption that there is an accident potential (AP) when environmental and human elements come into contact. To give a rather glib example; a raging white water river will not harm you whilst you sit on the bank, it is when you become involved with the river, through kayaking or canoeing, that there is an accident potential. This is shown by the two-circle model in figure xiv above. It is when the two elements, environmental and human, contain inherent dangers that the accident potential becomes greater and when there are a number of these elements that it is at its greatest.

For example on a kayaking trip the following elements might come into play;

Environmental	Human
rocks in river	inexperienced paddler
low water	old fibre glass kayak
bend in river	large group

It can be seen that in this example there is a large number of possible combinations which gives rise to a risky venture. Tight group control might alleviate some of the potential combinations but there are simply too many possible combinations to safely overcome in this case.

Accidents are often caused by lots of little things going wrong

DIFFERENT RISKS FOR DIFFERENT PEOPLE - Matching the risk to the individual

One of the most important things to remember about risk is that perceived risk is different for everybody and subjective risk is different for every group leader. What might be an impossibly dangerous activity for one instructor might be perfectly safe for a more experienced or better qualified instructor. Likewise every instructor is familiar with the student who cannot be persuaded that a high rope course is perfectly safe because he **perceives** it as dangerous whilst others members of the group are quite happy on the same obstacles. It is the difference in perceived risk that is discussed here. The difference in subjective risks is one which only experience, training and the judgement that comes with them can teach.

Remembering that one of the central components of the outdoor experience is that risk is used as a tool for self-development it follows that the level of perceived risk must be matched to the individual student for maximum effectiveness. (There is rarely any need, or justification, to increase the level of actual risk for individual students in a group situation)

Hopkins and Putnam (1993) refer to this need as the "problem of the match" and describe it as shown in figure xv. This Figure clearly shows that the potential for personal growth increases in line with the level of (perceived) risk until it reaches a stage where there is a dramatic fall off as the level of risk becomes too high. It is at this point where the potential for personal growth, or critical zone, is highest that outdoor leaders should be attempting to pitch their activities. The whole point of the problem of the match, and the reason why it is a problem, is that;

The match will be different for every member of a group

Some students may be scared of heights whilst others may be scared of water and yet others scared of the enforced sociability of the group environment. The mark of a really good outdoor instructor is that he or she will be able to pitch various activities at various levels so that everyone in the group will operate at some stage in the 'critical zone' with only an absolute minimum being bored by spending some time in the recreation zone and even less experiencing the misadventure zone. In an ideal world the whole group will constantly be moving between the adventure and critical zones throughout the duration of an outdoor course.

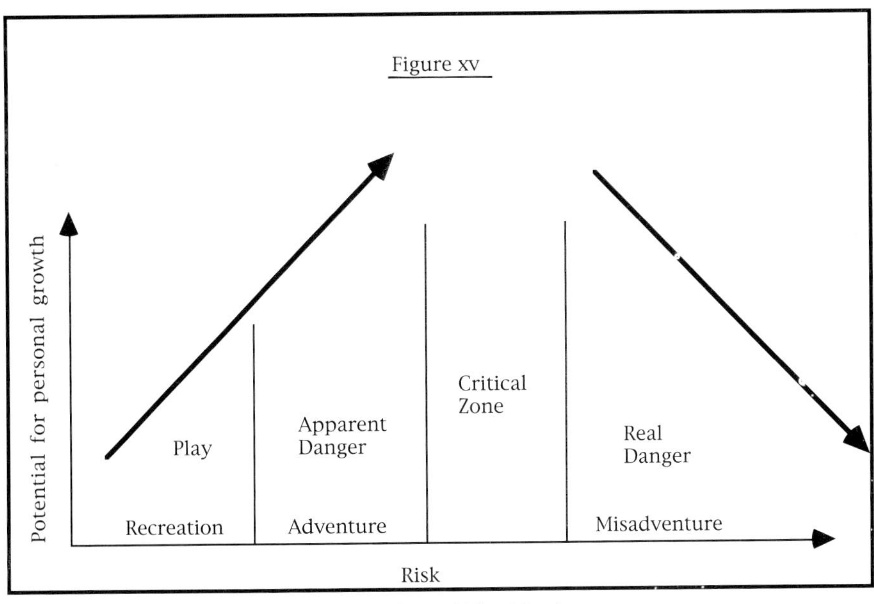

The Problem of The Match

Those people who have done much reading about outdoor education will instantly recognise that there is little new in Hopkins and Putnam's ideas. Rather they are based on the classic four stages of adventure first developed by Colin Mortiock (1984) these can be summarised as shown in figure xvi

In Mortlock's model, stage three, that of frontier adventure, equates with the critical zone in figure xv. As with Hopkins and Putnam, Mortlock makes the point that these stages will be different for each individual. What may be one person's play might easily be another person's misadventure.

A feature of Mortlock's stages of adventure is that they are clearly sequential with, for example, students needing to pass through the adventure stage of skills learning before moving into the higher risk of the frontier adventure stage.

Figure xvi

Stage one; PLAY

- Working at well below normal abilities.
- Minimal involvement.
- Fear of physical harm is absent.
- Response - range from 'fun/pleasant' to 'boring/waste of time'.

Stage two; ADVENTURE

- Feels in control but conscious of using abilities.
- Fear of physical harm is virtually absent.
- Progression stage/skills learning.

Stage three; FRONTIER ADVENTURE

- No longer in total control but able to succeed with effort/luck.
- Uncertain of outcome.
- Fear of physical harm and experience of psychological stress.
- Pride and satisfaction on completion.

Stage four; MISADVENTURE

- Beyond control.
- Fear and/or panic/terror.
- Possible high learning situation.

Mortlock's Stages of Adventure

The different levels, or stages, of adventure as developed by Mortlock and built on by Hopkins and Putnam can be represented by the following simple diagram in figure xvii developed by Tuson (1994).

Figure xvii

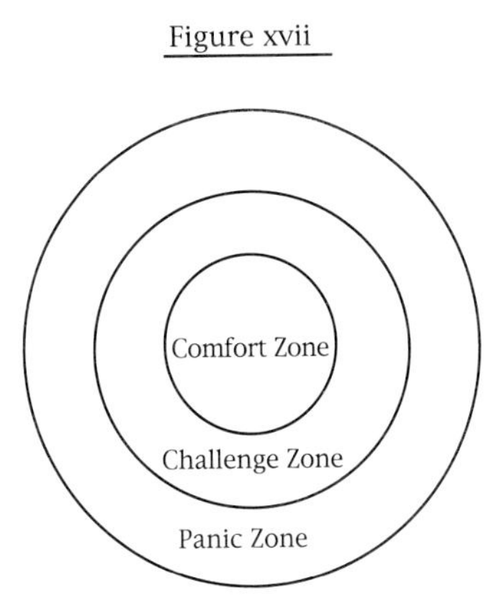

The zone model of adventure stages

In this model the objective is simply to keep the student within the challenge zone without going too far and entering the panic zone or being too complacent and allowing him to remain in the comfort zone. The challenge zone is elastic and can stretch or shrink depending on the students abilities and fears thus providing the match between activity and individual.

WHAT IS IT ALL ABOUT - The nature of risk.

There is a philosophical element to any discussion of risk, what cannot be denied in all this however is that there is also a very practical element. Risk in the outdoor environment can be summed up as all that is good in outdoor education and all that is bad. When attending an outdoor course students risk many things, some obvious and some not so obvious;

They risk **physical harm**, of all the risks involved in the outdoors this should be the one that an instructor can best keep under control. The difficulty is that if we go to the extreme and make outdoor courses 100% safe then our students risk **deception**. We cannot make outdoor courses purely perceived risk otherwise students might just as well go to Alton Towers, the outdoors is a risky environment.

More than most things, students risk the danger of **embarrassment**, providing that this doesn't get out of hand it is all part of a healthy learning experience. It is always worth remembering of course, that people have very different tolerance levels when it comes to being embarrassed. A major element in embarrassment is in the risk of being **vulnerable and open** which is an unnatural and awkward state for most people but one that is essential if true learning is to take place. A very real cause for concern, however, is the potential risk of **psychological harm** where emotions have gone too far, someone has been genuinely terrified or badly humiliated in a review. It goes without saying that such a situation is totally unacceptable. However psychological harm can be desperately hard to guard against, there are no safety ropes attached to a person's emotions. This is one area where all instructors need to be extra vigilant.

Many students, if not most, will find that they might well have to risk **facing up to their fears** and, even more daunting for many, risk **being honest with themselves** and take the greatest risk of **finding out something that they don't like about themselves.**

Perhaps if a course is badly written, badly run or simply fails to match expectations then a student stands to risk **time and money**. Whilst it is easy to be flippant about this it cannot be denied that outdoor courses can present a major investment in time and money for many students and that the investment is being made, more than anything else, in the instructor.

On the other hand if we do our job correctly then our students face the very real risk of **having fun** and **learning something.** Hopefully, if all these risks have been met and overcome, then the risk of **going home a changed person** is one we are all working towards.

"..... risks must be taken because the greatest hazard in life is to risk nothing,
the person who risks nothing does nothing, has nothing, is nothing,
They may avoid suffering and sorrow,
but they cannot learn, feel, change, grow, love or live.
Chained by their certainties they are slaves,
they have forfeited their freedom.
Only a person who risks is free"

5. THE KEY TO MOTIVATION

This chapter examines the major theories used in the study of motivation, particularly in work motivation. It starts with an explanation of the nature of motivation and the different 'schools' of motivation. It then takes a detailed look at Maslow's 'Hierarchy of Needs' which is treated as something of a special case because of its popularity. The chapter concludes with a summary of the theories of motivation that an instructor is most likely to come across, these include; 'Expectancy-Valence Theory', McGregor's 'X and Y Theory', Herzberg's 'Two-Factor Theory', 'Achievement Motivation', 'Attribution Theory' and 'Equity Theory'.

Instructor's need to have a basic grasp of these theories, not only because it will help on a personal level, but also because knowing them will help in relating the outdoor experience back to the workplace. In addition to this it is becoming more likely, with the increase in corporate work, that instructors will be asked to give presentations on basic motivational theory. This chapter is geared to these needs.

WHAT IS MOTIVATION - An introduction.

Although the study of motivation is a complex and sometimes bewildering subject, motivation itself can be simply described. This exact definition of motivation is one which has taken various forms as the science of psychology has progressed. The term 'motivation' itself has evolved from the Latin *movere*, meaning 'to move'. In a sense motivation can be taken as the force required to move, or drive, a person to take a particular action.

It is generally accepted, however, that motivation consists of more than just a simple drive. We now say that motivation is made up of three separate components which are referred to as **the motivation construct** (Steers and Porter, 1991) This consists of;

- How the behaviour is directed - the drive, or direction, component.
- How the behaviour is sustained - the persistence component.
- How the behaviour is energised - the vigour component.

There are, however, two 'schools' of motivation, those which deal with needs and those which deal with methods.

The former, those which deal with needs, are commonly referred to as the **'humanist'** school, this category is often seen as being exemplified by the eminent psychologist **Carl Rogers** (1964). These theories all deal with the internalised needs of people. A central belief of this school is that the most important determinants of human behaviour are inner qualities, notably a will to grow and develop towards fulfilment.

The second school of theory is one which deals with the processes used to encourage motivation and for this reason is often referred to as 'process theory' or the **'behaviourist'** school. This category of theory starts from the assumption that people can be motivated by extrinsic means, pay being the classic example. Much of process theory has been influenced by the work of **Ivan Pavlov** (1849-1936) who showed that dogs can be made to salivate at a neutral stimulus which had been associated with food. This response, known as 'a conditioned response' has generally become known as the basis of the 'carrot and stick' type of motivation exemplified by **B.F. Skinner** (1953).

Early theory, which was based on the behaviourist school, maintained that workers were essentially similar, being 'programmable' and showing a natural inclination to avoid work if possible. This theory and associated techniques, which came to be known as 'Scientific Management' after a term used by **F. W. Taylor** (1911) took away control over the task in hand from the workers and replaced it with a directive management style. Workers in this model were little more than a mindless resource who were controlled by economic needs and incentives.

The best summary of the difference between the two schools is given by **McGregor's X & Y Theory** (1957). Theory-X was seen by McGregor as the traditional management approach to the workforce in which they are regarded as lazy, do not like work and rather than looking for responsibility are geared towards finding security. In this scenario the workforce needs discipline, coercion and control to be effective. This theory, he maintained, is the basis for industrial conflict.

Theory-Y, however is the complete opposite of Theory-X. The workforce far from being workshy is essentially imaginative, responsible and hardworking. Whilst Theory-X suppresses workers, Theory-Y opens the way to greater productivity through ideas such as decentralisation and delegation, job enlargement, participation, consultative management and performance appraisal.

THE MOST POPULAR THEORY - Maslow's Hierarchy of Needs.

Perhaps because of its simple and elegant nature, one of the most popular motivation theories in use today is **Maslow's Hierarchy of Needs** (1943) This theory says that people have several layers of needs that need to be fulfilled starting with basic physical needs and moving up, through safety, social and esteem needs, to needs of growth and 'self-actualisation'. Self-actualisation is seen as the ultimate goal of a person who on reaching it becomes 'fully-functioning' in harmony with his own needs and feelings and at one with others. The classical model of Maslow's Hierarchy (Figure xviii) is the ascending pyramid.

Figure xviii

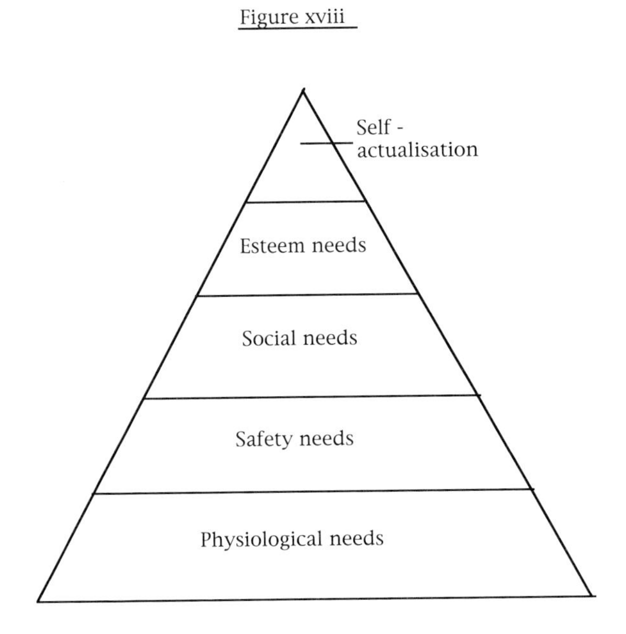

Maslow's Hierarchy of Needs

It has been suggested, however, that this traditional model implies that basic physiological needs are the greatest needs and that progressively higher needs are also progressively smaller and thus less important. This suggests that the pyramid would make more sense if it was reversed with the basic needs being the smallest, and therefore easiest to satisfy, whilst the higher needs becoming successively larger and more important. Whichever way up the pyramid goes it is, usually, important that lower level needs are fulfilled in order for a person to ascend to higher levels.

In terms of an outdoor course the lower two needs, physiological and safety, can be equated to such physical things as food, shelter, good equipment and safety procedures. The next two levels, of social and esteem needs, can be satisfied by the group environment, support and respect of peers and so on. Self-actualisation can be seen as the ultimate, and realistically unlikely, goal of an outdoor course where a student reaches his or her full potential.

Maslow's work is open to criticism on a number of fronts, notably that his work is vague and empirically unsound. The hierarchy of needs theory is based on a study of unnamed individuals many of whom were historical where he relied on written accounts of their lives. The second major criticism of the self-actualising school of thought, as exemplified by Maslow, is that it serves a small elite. It is apparent that people tied to routine work or confined by a lack of education or expectations will find the path proscribed by the Hierarchy of Needs virtually impossible.

THE POPULAR WORKPLACE THEORIES - A summary.

There are two popular theories which reflect the old-style 'scientific management' or behaviourist school of motivation, these are **equity theory** and **expectancy-valence theory**. This section also includes the contrasting **Two-factor Theory.**

Equity theory is often seen as the principle theory when discussing the 'fairness' of wages. One of the main attractions of this theory is that it has a firm 'common sense' basis which makes it easily understood by the layman. The basic assumption of equity theory is that employees seek fairness, or justice, in the employee-employer relationship. Perceived imbalances in this relationship, i.e. unfairness, are assumed to result in tension which cause staff to find ways of redressing this imbalance. Whilst an obvious employee tactic is to withhold their labour employee theft is a much larger problem with companies in which workers feel exploited. Theft is seen in this context as a way of addressing inequity.

Although equity theory has now been predominately overtaken by expectancy-valence theory it is still highly relevant to the argument about wages. According to

Adams (1963) who developed the theory, the ratio of a persons inputs and outcomes is balanced, by that person, against the equivalent ratio of the other person involved in the exchange or against a third person involved in a similar exchange. If these ratios are unequal then a state of inequity is said to exist.

Expectancy-valence theory works on the principle that people work (force) in return for desired, or expected outcomes (expectancy) usually of an economic or reward nature (valence). The theory is neatly summarised by the formula;

Force = Valence x Expectancy

In essence this theory says that workers will be motivated to put in as much effort as is needed to achieve what is perceived by them to be a desirable outcome. Expectancy-valence theory is still a powerful force in work motivation studies, particularly as it can be used as both an argument for and an argument against performance related pay. The principle of expectancy theory that people work for expected results, or incentives, would lead to the assumption that performance related pay works in theory. In reality, however, it is unlikely to because of the need to show that performance must be measurable and clearly attributed to the individual.

One of the most popular theories in use in the workplace today is **Herzberg's Two-Factor or Motivator-Hygiene Theory** (1968). In the same way as Maslow, Herzberg was very much of the humanist school of psychology in that he believed that the purpose of life, and work, is to move towards some concept of growth. This is reflected in his theory which states that the motivation factors in the workplace are those which encourage growth.

The Two Factor theory takes the stance that there are two factors in play (figure xvix) when considering the motivation of people in the workplace. These are **motivators** which are intrinsic to the job itself and **hygienes** or de-motivators which are extrinsic. He lists the basic growth or motivating factors as achievement, recognition, the work itself, responsibility and growth or advancement whilst de-motivating factors or hygienes are listed as company policy and administration, supervision, interpersonal relationships, working conditions, salary, status and security. His hygiene factors are associated with basic biological needs and drives, for example hunger is a basic biological drive which makes it necessary to earn money so money becomes a specific need. Motivator factors are those associated with job content whilst hygiene factors are associated with job environment.

Figure xvix

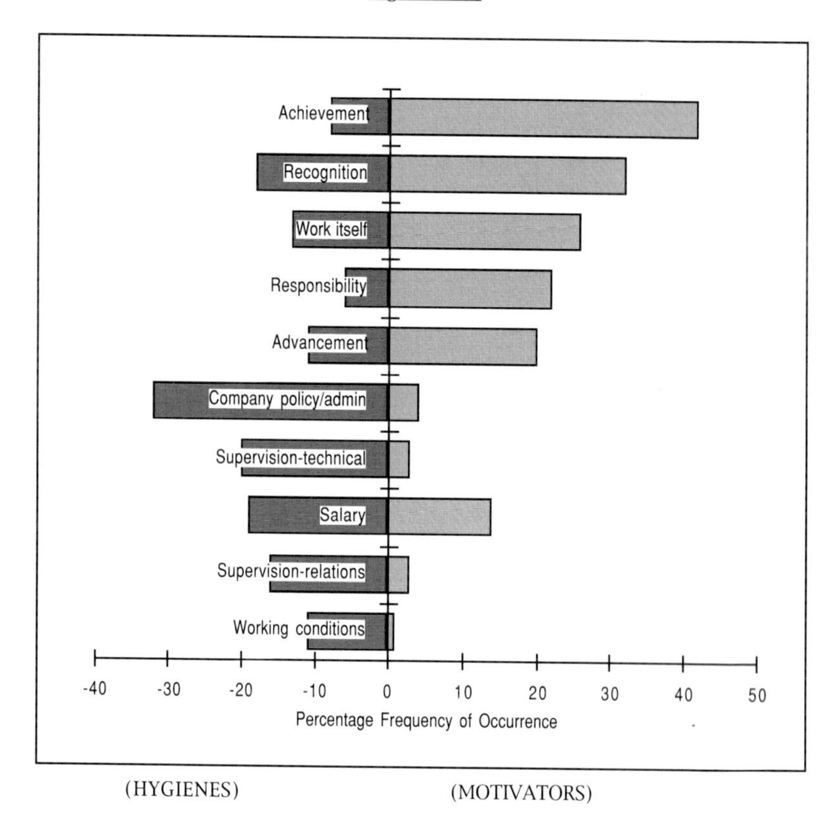

Comparison of Herzberg's motivators and hygienes.

The essence of Two Factor theory is that hygiene factors do not provide motivation in the workplace but a lack of them leads to de-motivation whilst motivators are motivating in their own right. It is important, however, to note that motivators and hygienes do not act exclusively as motivators and de-motivators. Figure xvix shows that they can also act in the opposite role, although in a more limited manner. For example whilst salary is a notable hygiene, i.e. its absence is a significant de-motivator, its presence can, to a smaller extent, act as a motivator.

Herzberg's conclusions were based on a series of interviews with 203 engineers and accountants based at nine plants or factories based in or around Pittsburgh. Each of the subjects was asked to identify periods in their history when their feelings about the job were markedly lower or higher than usual. This technique has led to the criticism that Herzberg's theory is similar to Maslow's Hierarchy in that it only really applies to a professional elite. Another major critique which has been levelled at Herzberg's methodology is in the structure of his interview questions which leads the interviewee to think in terms of opposites of good and bad. This brings in the concern that when people are asked to thing in this way, particularly with regard to extremes, that there is a natural tendency to think of the self as being responsible for the good items whilst external influences are responsible for the bad

THE MOTIVATION TO SUCCEED - Achievement and Attribution.

There are two main theories which look at peoples motivation to succeed, these are **Achievement Motivation Theory** and **Attribution Theory**. Achievement motivation theory, which was developed by McCelland (1961) says that people have three main needs;

- The need for achievement
- The need for affiliation
- The need for power

McCelland argued that most individuals have all of these needs but to highly varying greater or lesser extents. One of the most interesting points of this theory is that it states that the needs above are developed as a result of childhood experience and cultural background rather than of inherited factors.

People with a high need for achievement may display a tendency for success due to realistic goal setting but they are not noted as being good team members because of their need to exercise responsibility. The aspect of goal setting is a critical area of achievement theory and stipulates that whilst high need achievers will set realistic goals, low need achievers will set goals that are either too high or too low. This allows them to have either an excuse for failure or an excuse for easy success. Having obtained easy success the person with low achievement needs has no need to increase the level of future goals, thus avoiding the possibility of failure.

People who exhibit high affiliation needs are noted as good team workers who regard the social aspects of the workplace as highly important. In successful people however this need will rarely be dominant.

The need for power has been said to be the aim of all human activity. Whether this is true or not it is more certain that the need for power is the basis of managerial success. McCelland argued that there are two distinct variations of the need for power. Personal power is that where individuals exercise power for its own sake whereas social power is that where individuals are more concerned to exercise power in order to achieve the goals of an organisation. Managers who exercise a high need for power by itself can be counter productive in their relationships with others. However if combined with other needs, and in particular achievement needs, it can lead to highly productive results.

Attribution Theory, which was developed by Heider (1944) is highly relevant to workers where a degree of autonomy is required. Its main premise is that an individual needs to feel (attribute) that achieving a set goal was largely due to his or her efforts. Figure xx, which illustrates this, makes it quite clear that attribution is biased (thicker arrow) in the direction of internal attribution.

Figure xx

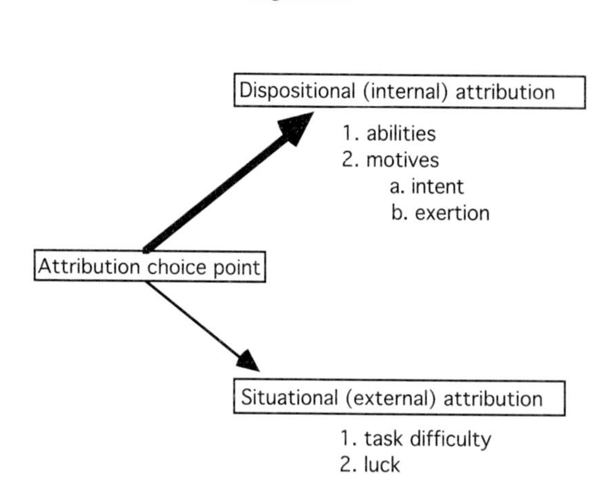

Heider's attribution model

Likewise, according to this theory people aim for success by carrying out tasks which they know are within their capabilities although for real feelings of success the activity needs to contain a suitable degree of challenge.

Rotter's (1954, cited in Weiner, 1974) Locus of Control Theory showed that the attributions highlighted in figure xx can be stable or unstable. Figure xxi which combines the elements of stability and instability with internal and external attributions is the widely seen model found in general use today.

The attribution model highlights the way in which success at a task is attributed by a person to internal and external factors, locus of control, and relates that to the expectancy, stability dimensions, of repeating that success. It can be seen, for example, that success gained through ability is a constant dimension and therefore engenders a high probability of being repeated. However if the external factor of difficulty is not right, for example it is too low and the task is accomplished easily, there will be no associated feeling of pride.

Figure xxi

STABILITY DIMENSIONS		Internal	External
	Stable	Ability	Task Difficulty
	Unstable	Effort	Luck

Attribution Theory Model (Adapted from Weiner, 1974)

The opposite of this is that if the task level is set at a very high level success may be attributed to luck. This being an unstable dimension there will be a low expectancy of future success. In a similar manner failure can also be associated with stable and unstable dimensions. Failure attributed to a perceived feeling of low effort being put into a task will, for example, possibly lead the person to believe that success is attainable in the future. Failure due to the task being too hard or through lack of ability, both stable dimensions, will lead the person to expect failure in future efforts.

"A winner never quits.
A quitter never wins"

6. BUILDING TEAMS

One of the most popular objectives of outdoor courses is that of team, or group, development, indeed it is often the only stated objective. This chapter looks at the characteristics of effective teams and the roles played within teams. It then looks at team development, the stages that teams go through and the barriers to that development. The chapter concludes by looking at how to maintain the team.

The development of teams can range from the simple 'bonding' weekend where a group of colleagues get together for a weekend of activities ranging from rock climbing to driving battle tanks in order to get to know each other better to the other extreme of very serious courses designed to address specific issues. The most notable of these issues will, almost inevitably include;

- Communication - inter personal and inter team/department
- Trust - between peers and between seniors/juniors
- Responsibilities - their acceptance and division
- Reward and praise - and criticism

It is important to recognise that in early discussion sessions many issues, especially communication and trust, will be put forward by a group as the expected cliché answers. It will take some time to get beyond this initial stage (see sections on communication and reviewing)

WHAT MAKES A TEAM - Characteristics of effective teams.

Bad teamwork is often characterised by an increase in **bureaucracy** usually with long chains of command and autocratic leadership. A result of this in the workplace is that personal territories and tasks are vigorously defended with accompanying feuds between departments, teams within departments and managers and departments. The ultimate result of all this is poor productivity with repeated and duplicated tasks and a poor, even hostile, working environment. This misplaced use of energy in a bad team is demonstrated by the team climate model of Vincent Nolan (1987) shown in figure xxii. This shows that, in a threatening or adversarial team, energy is wasted on emotional survival rather than completing the task.

<u>Figure xxii</u>

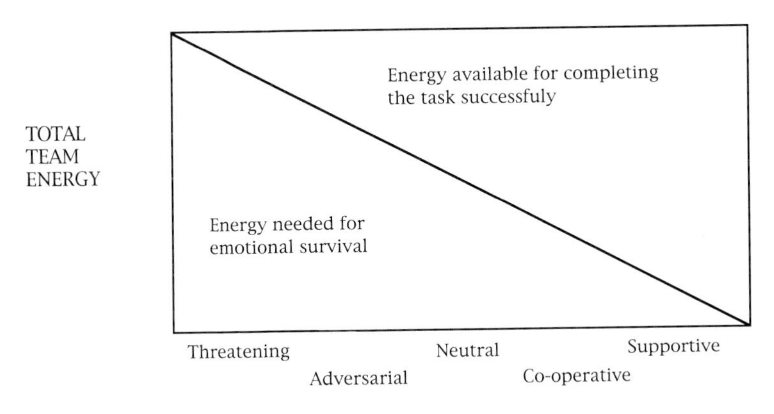

Team Climate Model

Team size has a significant effect on both team development and function. In an ideal world teams would be kept small enough to maintain close working links with effective, and open, communication but large enough to provide support and task effectiveness. In reality this will almost always end up as a compromise situation. What does seem certain is that teams which contain more than five or six members need to develop a more hierarchical system, with structured leadership, in order to be effective. It can be argued that the larger team which functions in total harmony by virtue of concord without the need for leadership is a myth. A debatable point, perhaps, but always a good one to put into a group discussion!

There are many lists of the features that constitute an effective team. The list below is a composite of the common features typically found on these lists, it is presented in no particular order.

- A clear and commonly shared vision of the purpose and aims of the team.
- Good communication within the team and with other teams, this includes good listening skills.
- Openness when confronting difficult issues and the support needed to make this possible.

- Consensus rather than compromise in decision making.

- Appropriate level of leadership together with support for the leadership and effective delegation of responsibilities.

- A willingness to confront traditional working practices.

- A willingness to accept help, both from within and without the team together with high levels of co-operation.

- High levels of mutual trust especially across the various levels of seniority.

- Constant development of the team and individuals within it.

- Regular reviews of technical and personnel/personal issues.

- A willingness to use creative conflict, rather than aimless and destructive competition.

- Efficient and commonly agreed decision making procedures and working practices.

- The ability to adapt to change, including accepting new team members.

- And finally - useful meetings rather than endless talking in circles!

WHAT TEAM MEMBERS DO - Team roles.

If there is one psychological test/computer programme which is used more than any other on team building courses it is that developed by Meredith Belbin (1981) As with many of these models it is perhaps more widely used than understood. In essence, through a series of tick box questions, it identifies a number of team roles which Belbin maintains are needed to build an effective team. These roles are shown in figure xxiii. The Belbin test is typically done by the individual, in other words the results are how a person sees themselves, it can be done with people ticking the boxes for their fellow team members but this is unusual and may be problematic.

Figure xxiii; *Belbin's team roles*

	Characteristics	Contribution	Weaknesses
Plant	• Creative • Imaginative • Unorthodox	• Solves difficult problems	• Ignores incidentals • Pre-occupied • Poor communicator
Resource Investigator	• Extrovert • Enthusiastic • Communicative	• Explores opportunities • Develops contacts	• Over-optimistic • Loses interest easily
Co-ordinator	• Mature • Confident	• Clarifies goals • promotes decision making • Good at delegating	• Offloads own work • Can be taken as manipulative
Shaper	• Challenging • Dynamic • Works well under pressure	• Overcomes obstacles • Pushes ideas through	• Easily provoked • Can offend other people
Monitor Evaluator	• Sober • Discerning	• Sees strategic picture • Sees all options • Good judge of options	• Fails to inspire others • Can be seen to lack drive
Teamworker	• Co-operative • Mild personality • Perceptive and diplomatic	• Builds team • Averts friction • A good listener	• Indecisive under pressure
Implementer	• Disciplined • Reliable and efficient	• Turns ideas into actions	• Inflexible • Conservative • Slow to respond
Completer	• Painstaking • Conscientious	• Delivers on time • Searches out errors and mistakes	• Inclined to worry • Bad at delegating
Specialist	• Dedicated • Single-minded • Self-sufficient	• Provides specialist knowledge and skills	• Dwells on technical issues • Only contributes on technical points

What is often missed by many of those using the Belbin model, and test, is that the roles identified are volatile, they are not fixed. This is an important point because all too often students on courses are told they are, for example, predominately a 'resource investigator' and led to believe that this is their fixed personality. This is not the case; a person's role can change through such developments as education, experience, promotion, maturity and so on. In addition to this all people will play a number of different roles to a greater or lesser degree and few people will be characterised by one or two roles at the expense of all the others.

Although Belbin has become almost an industry standard, the awkward terms he uses to describe some of the team roles means that simpler terms are often used to describe team roles. These can be purely task oriented roles, for example co-ordinator, time-keeper, record keeper and so on or they can reflect Belbin's ideas using such terms as thinker, worker, leader and resource controller. Likewise negative terms can be applied to such people as the shirker, criticiser, dominator or trouble maker. The difficulty with many of these terms is in the application, using anonymous cards can be one technique to label team members after an exercise but whilst this may protect those doing the describing, the feelings of those being described can still be badly hurt. One of the joys of the Belbin test is that no-one else need be involved.

TEAM DEVELOPMENT - The stages.

Perhaps the most popular model of team development in use today is that developed by John Jones (1973) which maintains that teams go through four notable stages, of **Forming, Storming, Norming** and **Performing** as shown in figure xxiv.

One of the most important things to remember with the Jones model is that the stages are volatile in both directions - it is just as possible to slip backwards as it is to go forwards. This change is usually most apparent when team members, especially senior members, or the task changes. In reality few teams function for more than a short moment in the performing stage. It is more likely that established teams will operate for the majority of time in the norming stage with occasional short moves towards the stages above and below that.

Some models place another stage, that of **Re-forming**, between norming and performing. This stage allows for the issues raised during the previous stages to be addressed before the team can function effectively. A final stage, **Dis-banding**, is also sometimes added but this is not, strictly speaking, a stage in team development.

Figure xxiv; *The Stages Of Team Development*

Forming (immature team or ritual sniffing) sometimes termed - **undeveloped** team.	• Considerable anxiety • Testing to discover the nature of the group • The leader is looked to for decisions • Low levels of productivity • Questions are asked about what is appropriate behaviour • Communication is at a polite level • Expectations are raised about the future The team needs - structure, leadership and standards
Storming (fractionated team) sometimes termed - **experimenting** team.	• Opinions become polarised • Authority/the leader is questioned and challenged • Communication is characterised by argument • There is a dip in morale and disillusionment with expectations • Team members jostle for superiority and clear roles The team needs - resolution of conflicts and agreement regarding tasks and team roles
Norming (sharing team) sometimes termed - **consolidating** team.	• The team becomes comfortable and possibly complacent • Communication is based around an open exchange of ideas • There is support and co-operation amongst team members • Plans and standards are agreed • Team members are careful not to upset others in order to avoid a return to the storming stage • Productivity is reasonable but not high or effective The team needs - greater interdependence and task focus together with the confidence to face up to conflict issues
Performing (effective team) sometimes termed - **mature** team.	• Team energy is applied to the task rather than personnel issues • There are feelings of pride and eagerness • Team members are capable of both interdependent and independent action • The team is clearly structured in an appropriate manner • Roles are defined and yet remain flexible The team needs - an awareness of itself in order not to slip back into the norming stage

THE PROBLEMS WITH TEAMS - Barriers to development.

A badly developed team is more than just the opposite of a good team, there are additional barriers which may act to prevent the development of teams. Many of these barriers will appear on team development courses and will need to be addressed either through review and discussion or through more direct techniques such as 'gagging' key team members during certain tasks. This list is based on the work of Rosabeth Moss Kanter (1984)

- External status is transferred into the course setting, this is where a manager in the workplace either acts as the manager on the course or, sometimes even worse, is treated by the course participants as the team leader. Where the course is being run to address issues found within the workplace this is not always a problem, but this is rare.

- There is a knowledge gap within the team. In simple, and simplistic, terms this is often manifested on courses by the ex-scout phenomenon. This is where the male ex-scouts tie all the knots and build the raft whilst the female non ex-scouts feel intimidated by the seemingly knowledgeable activity being undertaken and therefore decline to play any role other than observer. There can also be much deeper different levels of people, thinking and communication skills which need to be overcome.

- Sub-groups exist within the team. Again, in simplistic terms, this can be as simple as all the smokers sticking together because they are forced to take their breaks outside of the review room. Almost any sub-group will tend to be counter-productive.

- There is rivalry between team members. It has been known for career prospects or even future employment to depend on performance on a course. This is, however, highly destructive and thankfully rare. Rivalry and power politics are only natural amongst any group of people and can result in healthy competition as well as disruption.

- There are underlying tensions within the team. These can be particularly difficult to handle because the course leader will be totally unaware of their cause and sometimes even their very existence. Clues such as a blatant reluctance of two people to work together may indicate a history of conflict which will need to be resolved, preferably by the people involved.

- The myth of 'the team'. This is where a team believes, or is led to believe, that it is some kind of super team. Managers pep talks are a good example of this where underlying problems are swept aside by a deluge of rhetoric leaving the team unable to face its real difficulties.

- There is unrealistic bonding. The opposite to the myth of the team is where the team has bonded to an unhealthy degree leaving people unable to express true feelings, particularly about each other, for free of upsetting the team spirit. This is often seen where the team is asked to rate each others performance and each team member is given the same score.

THE KEY TO TEAMWORK - Decision making.

The essence of team work is that a group of people are working towards a common goal and each member of a team has a clearly defined role to play in reaching that goal. Before a team can reach this stage, however, it usually has to go through the hardest part of team work - arriving at decisions. Often the hardest decision can even be about the method to be used in making decisions! Completion of the task itself can sometimes be an anti-climax after the team has spent ages trying to decide on, often very trivial, procedures and designs. The following are the main types of decision making techniques. It is possible for a course leader to insist on a particular technique being used but it is usually best to allow a technique to adopted by the team and then examine its effectiveness in a subsequent review session.

- **Decision by lack of response.** In this technique ideas are suggested and rejected in turn until an idea is proposed which is not objected to and is therefore adopted. The decision making process is essentially a negative one with ideas being rejected and the danger of associated hurt feelings on the part of their proposers.

- **Decision by authority.** Can either be through an elected leader making autonomous decisions or through group discussion with a chairperson having the final say or casting vote. Whilst highly efficient this technique can lead to team members feeling that they have been removed from ownership of the decision and therefore from a need to play a part in the task.

- **Decision by agreement.** The perfect and most unlikely form of decision making is where everybody truly agrees with the course of action being proposed.

- **Decision by railroading.** This is not the same as decision by authority it is often carried out by not allowing any dissenting voices to be held through such tactics as the quick vote or the suggestion that 'if no-one objects lets get started' style of suggestion. This technique often comes about because of a bad, domineering, leadership style (see the chapter on leadership)

- **Decision by majority vote.** Usually done as either a first 'lets get the decision over with' ploy or as a last resort when a decision cannot be reached by other means. It's main hurdle is, of course, that the minority who voted against the motion will feel alienated from the subsequent action.

- **Decision by consensus.** Probably the most time-consuming but most acceptable technique of reaching a decision. As opposed to voting in this technique the case for a particular action is argued until everyone agrees with it or are at least happy to support it. The key to consensus is a team where everybody is able to express their own opinions and ideas without risk of confrontation.

- **Decision by compromise.** May often appear to be decision by consensus and usually arises from attempts to reach consensus but is in reality where somebody has agreed merely in order to bring the discussion to an end. This can be dangerous because resentments can be secretly built up.

There is no right or wrong way to reach a decision, just as there is no right or wrong style of leadership. The technique used will vary and depend on the situation, the nature of the team and many other external and internal considerations.

HOW A TEAM SURVIVES - Maintenance and needs of the team.

And finally - an effective team will have a number of needs in order to continue operating. The needs below are based on the list identified by John Jones (1973) and consist of;

The need for diversity, a team is made up of individuals. Not only will each individual have weak points they will also have strengths and skills. For a team to operate at maximum effectiveness these individual strong points need to be not only encouraged and utilised but as diverse as possible in order to give depth and breadth to the team.

The need for safety, fear and suspicion can come from both within and without the team, both are a barrier to effective operation. The team needs to provide a safe environment from which to accept and face challenges. This can only be done if trust, respect and openness exists between team members.

The need for shared commitment, is not about individual motivation but rather about a shared aim, purpose and vision. A shared commitment and strength of purpose will be needed most when the end goal of a task becomes lost or blurred. Without the shared commitment of a successful team individuals will go their own way and conflict will arise when difficulties arise.

The need for team identity, reflects the need within the vast majority of people for belonging. Team identity is reflected in integrity and perseverance to maintain standards in the face of difficulties. Team members need to be proud of their team and have not only a sense of belonging but also a sense of shared ownership.

The need for continuous development, just as individuals so too do teams need to develop and change. A team must be prepared to take new risks, accept new truths, roles and agendas or it will stagnate, become inflexible and, eventually, redundant.

In addition to these needs the 'perfect team' will still need maintenance in order to keep it that way. This can be done in a number of ways, notably through;

Encouraging	giving praise and reassurance
Harmonising	resolving disputes and the easing of conflict
Gate-keeping	making sure all team members have a role
Standard setting	setting rules of conduct and behaviour
Following	actively going along with team strategy

"Coming together is a beginning,
keeping together is progress,
working together is success."

7. HELP WITH PROBLEM SOLVING

Whilst there are no great theories here connected with the process of problem solving there are a number of established procedures and techniques which can be useful tools. This chapter is based on the most popular of these.

The key features of any successful problem solving team may appear to be contradictory. The team needs to be **analytical, logical, creative** and **innovative**. This underlines the importance of diversity within a team as discussed in the team development chapter.

WHAT NEEDS TO BE DONE - Problem solving responsibilities

There are a number of responsibilities which have to be fulfilled in order to successfully solve a problem. These responsibilities can be individual or collective, formal or informal, they are;

Information collecting. No problem can be solved unless it is known what the problem is and what are the conditions, time, equipment, etc. connected to that task. Surprisingly this is the task that is usually done badly with groups rushing into an activity without having all the information they need. This can be overcome by;

Confirming. Not only should it be confirmed that all the information needed is available but it is also needs to be confirmed that every member of the team is aware of that information. The problem needs to be completely clarified at this stage.

Suggesting and sharing. Often known as 'brainstorming' this is where strategies for solving the problem are discussed and a potential solution confirmed.

Co-ordinating. It is important to ensure that not only does each individual member of the team have a role but that each of those individuals and the sub-groups in which they are working are aware of their place and function within the overall scheme. These sub-groups, individuals and their associated functions will need to be co-ordinated in order to get them to link together.

Orientating. Building on the co-ordinating responsibility is a need to ensure that specific actions are carried out by specific people at selected places and times.

Evaluating. There will always be a need to have ongoing monitoring, evaluation, re-evaluation and constructive criticism to ensure that unforeseen problems are dealt with and new challenges are met.

HOW PROBLEMS ARE SOLVED - The problem solving process

Figure xxv

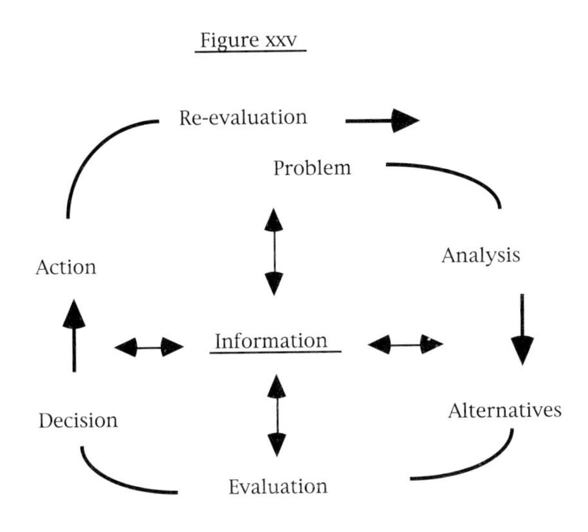

The Problem Solving Loop

The problem solving process is a reflection of not only the responsibilities outlined above but also the nature of the problem and the resources available to meet the problem. There does tend to be, however, a fairly standard process for solving problems which can be represented as the problem solving loop shown in figure xxv.

Although the loop consists of seven stages it is immediately apparent that information is the central factor in each stage. This emphasises the importance of the information collecting responsibility described above. The features of each stage in the problem solving loop are described below.

Problem. As much information as possible about the problem is gathered.

Analysis. The information is examined and confirmed in detail.

Alternatives. A number of alternative solutions are suggested and developed.

Evaluation. Each alternative is examined in turn and its pros and cons debated.

Decision. An alternative is chosen on its merits (see team decision making)

Action. Work commences on the chosen solution.

Re-evaluation. As work progresses the solution is monitored to ensure that it is fulfilling the criteria and adaptations made where necessary.

Obviously in addition to these stages there will need to be practical developments such as designating roles and responsibilities, collecting resources and so on. The loop does however give an elegant and simple model which can be used as a generic strategy for any problem.

The final stage which is not shown on the loop because it follows the decision making process is **evaluation** where the process is examined in hindsight either in the form of a review or as a critique of the exercise in preparation for the next task.

WHEN IT DOESN'T WORK - The difficulties in problem solving

It may be that even if the correct procedures are followed there are still difficulties with a team being unable to arrive at solutions for problems or, alternatively, not being able to follow those solutions through. These difficulties can be collected into five main areas or blocks, they are;

- **Technical.**

    - Not being methodical
    - Not understanding the problem
    - Mis-interpreting the problem
    - Using inappropriate techniques
    - Not having enough information
    - Not ensuring correct implementing of solution

- **Perceptual.**
    - Stereotyping
    - Mistaking cause and effect
    - Seeing what you expect, or want, to see
    - Not recognising that you are having difficulties
- **Intellectual.**
    - Lack of knowledge or skill
    - Inflexible
    - Lack of creativity
    - Not being methodical
- **Emotional.**
    - Impatience
    - Lack of real challenge
    - Fear of taking risks
    - Fear of making mistakes
    - Fear of embarrassment
- **Expressive.**
    - Inadequate information
    - Management too dominant or too passive
    - Language, usually technical, difficulties

These blocks can generally be overcome by;

- Observing and listening to fellow team members
- Ongoing monitoring, reviews and comparisons
- Rewards and recognition
- Open and free communication
- Sensible delegation
- Lack of conflict and avoidance of confrontation
- Showing commitment to innovation
- Supportive team members
- Giving ideas credit and avoiding criticism

8. THE SECRET OF REVIEWING

Reviewing can be seen in two ways both of which have their devoted supporters. Firstly it can be argued that the outdoor experience is totally self-contained and needs no elaboration. This was certainly the argument of the early educationalists who believed that 'the experience was everything' and talking about it was a waste of time. The second argument is that the outdoor experience is nothing unless it is discussed, analysed and related back to everyday life. It is this discussion, it is argued, which gives the outdoor experience its meaning. The reality is, of course, that the answer lies between these two camps. Too much talking can detract from the experience whilst no talking can render it meaningless. What is certainly true, however, is that reviewing done badly can at best be a waste of time and at worst can be extremely harmful.

Reviewing serves many purposes. Amongst these are practical reasons such as how could a task be improved on and discussing issues raised during an activity. Reviews can also be deeper and used to explore emotions or strong feelings. For the purpose of many outdoor courses, however, reviews are used to firstly make sense of, and develop, what has just happened in an activity and secondly to carry the lessons learnt forward into the next activity, everyday life, the workplace or life development. In a rather simplistic sense reviews exist to make people think.

This chapter deals with some of the main myths of reviewing as well as basic rules and some simple techniques. It is not intended as an all-inclusive guide to reviewing technique, there are now a number of good books on the subject which can usually be obtained from 'Adventure Education' in Penrith, tel; 01768-891065.

WHY PEOPLE DON'T REVIEW - Reviewing myths.

There are many myths surrounding reviewing, these are some of the more common;

The review is the serious bit of the course. The idea that reviewing needs to consist of a group of people sitting in a circle earnestly discussing the meaning of life is not only wrong it is responsible for more bad reviews than almost anything else. **Reviews can be fun!**

The review takes place at the end of an activity. There is no need for a review to take place at the end of a session or activity, it can take place after, during or even before (this is called **front-loading**) a session.

The review needs to be a formal session. Nothing could be further from the truth, there is no need for reviews to be formal. Holding a review over dinner whilst sitting around the camp fire can be far more productive than sitting around a table. Likewise a purely informal sharing of the days highlights with lots of loud voices and laughter can not only be a great review it can also be a great way to end a day.

The review involves the whole group. Often it may be simply inappropriate to involve the whole group. Asking a small sub-group why they are watching an activity rather than taking part can lead to a valuable on the spot review which may salvage an entire course.

The review is all about talking. Some of the best reviews involve little or even no talking. Don't be afraid to use drawing, acting or mime to explore themes, often people are more comfortable with using mediums other than talking.

Each activity needs reviewing. There will be times when the group is so active and on such a high that to force them to stop and discuss what is happening could stop the flow. Save the ideas, note them down perhaps, and review later if this is happening.

A review should have a set finishing time. There are mixed views on this. Certainly some people, if allowed, will happily talk all night and perhaps they do need some structure or a time limit setting. However if genuinely useful or important ideas are being raised then it may be a mistake to finish because the clock says so. Another danger with setting a time is that some people may not get a chance to speak or even worse they may emotionally open themselves up and then be left hanging with no conclusion to the discussion.

Reviewing is difficult. Whilst reviewing should not be thought of as easy it is nothing to be scared of. Following a few simples guidelines, such as the four stage reviewing technique described below, can make all the difference. Reviewing is, however, a skill and needs to be learnt in exactly the same way as belaying a climber or paddling a kayak.

Reviews are emotional. People should not be forced to reveal their deepest emotions just because a misguided reviewer believes that the review is a failure unless everyone is in tears. Some reviews will be emotional but there is no need for every review to be so, indeed it will often be completely inappropriate.

EFFECTIVE REVIEWING- A few basic rules.

Every activity needs some rules and reviewing is no different. Many of the rules are in reality guidelines but they should be adhered to unless there is a good reason why not. Many of these rules can be put forward to the group as 'ground-rules' for a review session.

Reviews are confidential. In some review situations people will reveal their feelings, emotions and history more than is usual. Anything that is revealed in this way should be regarded as confidential just as if it was in a counselling session or a medical interview. Obviously some reviews are designed to be shared with outsiders, a good example being the end of course review where lessons are learnt for future courses.

Reviewing demands respect. There can be few things worst in life than being laughed at or put down when putting forward a contribution to a discussion. Everyone in the review group has an absolute right to be listened to with respect.

A review is not for someone to show off their knowledge. There is a danger, particularly, for younger instructors, to use review sessions to show how clever they are. When someone starts spouting off theories and ideas without input from the rest of the group it becomes a lecture not a review.

Everyone has an opinion. A review must not be monopolised by one or two people, there should be an opportunity for anyone, who wants to, to speak. Even more importantly other group members need to **listen** to their opinions.

No-one can be forced to give an opinion. If someone does not want to speak they should not be forced to. Hopefully the group will be supportive enough that no-one feels too intimidated to speak.

Reviews should be positive. Although not everything that happens during an activity or a course will be positive it is important that the review does more than just highlight negative features. No-one, or group, should ever be knocked down if they are not then picked back up. If it is at all possible every review should end on a positive note even if it is only 'well; we are all agreed that was rubbish but at least we know why it was so bad. So now we can improve on it by using those lessons we've just learnt'.

The reviewer needs to be responsive. In the ideal world the reviewer will not force opinions or lead groups into discussions. He will rather respond to the group's needs and allow them to draw out lessons and issues. Although the reviewer may have to keep a session 'on track' he should be stimulating discussion rather than leading it.

A SIMPLE TECHNIQUE - Four stage reviewing.

A useful framework to base a review on is that suggested by Roger Greenaway (1996) Not everyone will like the idea of such a formal framework but it is important in even the most informal and 'on the hoof' review to have a clear idea of what you are doing. The four stage sequence is one technique for doing that. It is not suggested here that the framework is adhered to rigidly with allocated time slots for each stage, but rather it is used as a guideline. Based on the learning cycle, it consists of **Experience, Express, Examine** and **Explore** stages.

The experience stage, concentrates on **what happened?** It can be likened to gathering evidence to serve as a reminder. Often a good way of doing this is for people to talk through what they felt happened, this often leads to other group members being surprised at how others perceived the same incidents.

The express stage, asks **how did it feel?** This stage is a vital one but can often be glossed over because of time constraints or because group members are finding it difficult to express their emotions.

The examine stage, is the analytical stage which asks **what do you think?** and seeks to rationalise what happened. Inexperienced reviewers sometimes tend to jump straight to this stage in an attempt to keep the 'buzz' of the activity going - this is usually a mistake.

The explore stage, is more practical and asks **what next?** This stage applies the lessons learnt from the experience and moves them forward or translates them into some meaning in everyday life.

AIDS TO REVIEWING - Some hints.

Whilst this chapter is not an all inclusive guide to reviewing there are some techniques which it is worth being aware of.

Front-loading. Some people may not regard this as a review technique because it comes before an activity but it is all part of the ongoing review process. In essence it consists of asking questions such as 'what are we going to do?' 'how are we going to do it?' 'what do we need to bear in mind?' 'what fears do people have about doing this?' and so on. A front-loading session can follow a very similar format to an end of session review but with the added bonus that people will be thinking about the issues whilst doing the activity thereby having more to contribute to a later review session. Questions and issues (Priest and Gass, 1994) that might be raised by frontloading include;

- **Revist** - what lessons where learnt from the last activity
- **Objectives** - what is the aim of the next activity and what can be learnt from it
- **Motivation** - why is the activity important and how does it relate to everyday life
- **Function** - what behaviour and actions will help to bring about success and how best to use them
- **Dysfunction** - what behaviour and actions will hinder success and what to do about them.

The use of metaphor. Metaphors have many uses but their main purpose is to provide a platform for relating the outdoor experience back to the everyday life of the students. Metaphors can be immediately obvious such as 'we are going to build a raft which is similar to putting together a project back in the workplace' or more subtle such as the old favourite 'climbing a mountain is like life itself, sometimes you have to get through the clouds to see where you are going'. Metaphors used in this way can be extremely powerful, they can also be extremely silly if used constantly and inappropriately.

Metaphors can also be used for individual descriptions, for example 'if you were a car/tree/plant/house/etc. what would you be and why?' might produce the answer 'I would be a Volvo because I like to think of myself as steady and dependable'. The same technique can also be used to get group members to describe each other which is often a very effective way of overcoming peoples embarrassment at talking about each other.

Physical reviewing. This means that people actually move to express their feelings. Physical reviewing can be a fun way of getting people involved who might otherwise sit there in silence. It can be as simple as standing up to express happiness and sitting down to express sadness. It can also be more complex with people moving around to stand in different places to show their feelings. For example, an outline of a swimming pool can be laid out with people standing in the 'deep end' to show they are fully involved or standing in the 'shallow end' to signify that they are unsure of committing themselves. Obviously such an activity requires a large amount of individual interpretation, standing at the 'deep end', for example, may signify to some people that they are out of their depth!

The use of drama. Drama can be a lot of fun, particularly for children who can act out a situation rather than siting around and describing it. The drama need not be a literal report of an event, a group might be asked to provide a dramatic interpretation of lessons learnt during an activity. In this way the review itself becomes another activity.

Drawing. The type of drawing need not be a picture, it might be in the form of a map showing the 'journey' undertaken during an activity or it could consist of symbolic pictures each with a theme. The effectiveness of this type of reviewing is shown by its popular use as a form of counselling and therapy.

Chuff charts. Often known as 'highs and lows' this simply entails going through an activity and scoring moments during it on certain criteria such as how scary or how much fun. This technique can be very effective if group members do their own chuff charts and then compare them followed by a discussion of the differences.

About the author;

Peter Barnes currently works at the University of Strathclyde where, amongst other things, he is completing his Ph.D. in 'The motivation of staff in the outdoor industry'. In addition to a number of private outdoor centres and management training companies he is mainly associated with Outward Bound having worked at the Wales, Ullswater, Hong Kong and Sabah schools. A keen caver and mountaineer, Peter lives in Penrith, Cumbria.

REFERENCES;

Adair, J. (1988) The Action-Centred Leader

Adams, J, S. (1963) 'Towards an understanding of inequity.' IN Journal of Abnormal and Social Psychology Vol. 67, pp. 422-436

Belbin, R, M. (1981) Managing Teams - Why they succeed or fail

B.T. (1997) Talkworks

Csikszentmihayli, M. (1990) Flow

Dewey, J. (1938) Experience and Education

Greenaway, R. (1996) Reviewing Adventures, Why and How

Heider, F. (1944) 'Social perception and phenomenal causality' IN Psychological Review Vol. 51,

Herzberg, F. (1968) Work and the Nature of Man

Hopkins, D. and Putnam, R. (1993) Personal Growth Through Adventure

Jones, J, E. (1973) 'A model of group development' IN Jones, J, E. and Pfeiffer, J, W. The annual handbook for group facilitators

Kanter, R, M. (1984) Change Masters

Kolb, D, A. et al (1971) Organisational Psychology - An Experimental Approach

Luft, J. (1961) 'The Johari Window' IN Human Training News Vol. 5 (1)

Maslow, A. H. (1943) A Theory of Human Motivation

Maslow, A. (1959) New Knowledge in Human Values

McClelland, D. (1961) The Achieving Society

McGregor, D. M. (1957) 'The Human side of Enterprise.' IN Adventures in Thought and Action.

Priest, S. (1990) 'Thoughts on managing dangers in Adventure Programmes' IN Journal of Adventure Education and Outdoor Leadership (JAEOL) Vol. 13(1)

Priest, S & Gass, M. (1994) 'Frontloading with paradox and double binds in adventure education facilitation' IN JAEOL Vol. 11(1)

Mortlock, C. (1984) The Adventure Alternative

Nolan, V. (1987) Teamwork

Rogers, C. (1964) On Becoming a Person

Skinner, B. F. (1953) Science and Human Behaviour.

Steers, R, M. and Porter, L, W. (1991) Motivation and Work Behaviour

Tannerbum, R. & Schimdt, W. (1968) 'How to choose a leadership pattern' IN Harvard Review

Taylor, F. W. (1911) Principles of Scientific Management.

Tuson, M. (1994) Outdoor Training For Employee Effectiveness

Weiner, B, M. (1974) Achievement Motivation and Attribution Theory

Wharton (1996) 'Health and safety in outdoor activity centres' IN JAEOL Vol. 12(4)